DIARY LEAVES

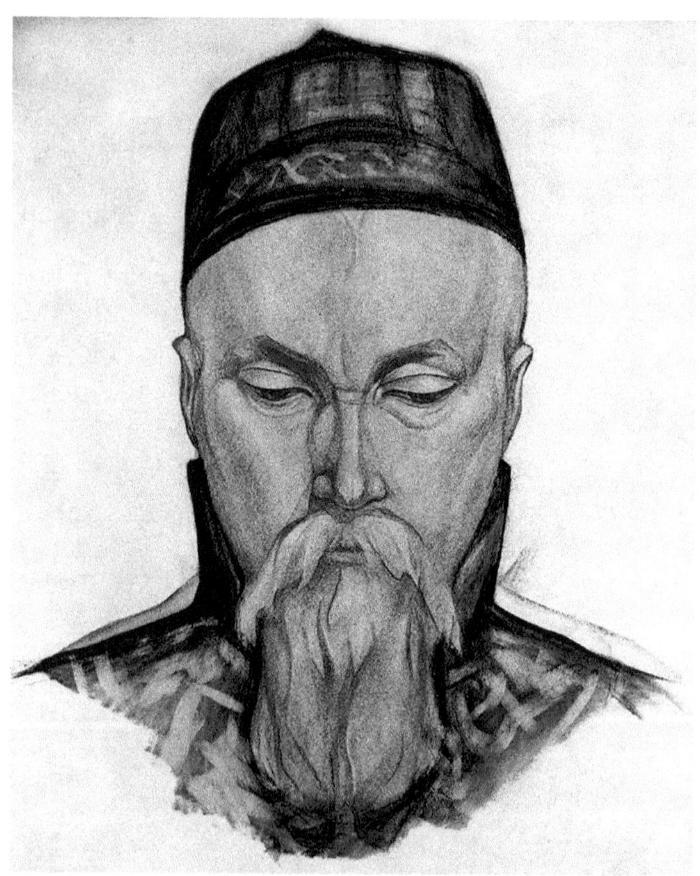

Portrait of Nicholas Roerich by Svetoslav Roerich

DIARY LEAVES

NICHOLAS ROERICH

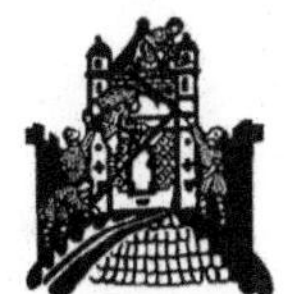

NICHOLAS ROERICH MUSEUM

NEW YORK   MMXXI

Nicholas Roerich Museum
319 West 107th Street
New York NY 10025
www.roerich.org

Cover illustration: Nicholas Roerich. *Himalayas.* 1933.

PUBLISHER'S NOTE

DIARY LEAVES is the last book of the *Nicholas Roerich: Collected Writings* series, comprising a collection of his articles, which were published from 1921 to 1947 in periodicals of India, the UK and the USA.

Nicholas Roerich is known to many as a painter. His paintings, of which there are thousands around the world, explore the mythic origins, the natural beauty, and the spiritual strivings of humanity and of the world. But Nicholas Roerich was as prolific a writer as he was a painter. He wrote many articles, books, poetry, and almost-daily essays on life and events, which he called 'diary leaves'.

Many of these writings have been unavailable for decades. They will therefore be new to many readers. It is our hope that volumes of the *Nicholas Roerich: Collected Writings* series will expand awareness of the vast range and depth of Roerich's interests and insights into human nature and cultural history.

We would like to thank all those who helped in the preparation of the books of the *Nicholas Roerich: Collected Writings* series, and without whom its publication would not have been possible. Our special thanks go to Jean Fletcher, Laraine Lippe, Kathryn Agrell, Kathy O'Conner and Joleen Dianne DuBois.

CONTENTS

CONTENTS

DIARY LEAVES

BEAUTY AND WISDOM

From a lecture to the young generation,
read in London on December 14th, 1919

[*The Theosophical Path*, No. 2, February, 1921, pp. 187–193]

TO the sacred ideals of nations in our days, the watchwords "Art and Knowledge" have been added with special imperativeness. It is just now that something must be said of the particular significance of these great conceptions, both for the present time and for the future. I address these words to those whose eyes and ears are not yet filled with the rubbish of everyday life, to those whose hearts have not yet been stopped by the lever of the machine called "mechanical civilization."

Art and Knowledge! Beauty and Wisdom! It is not necessary to speak of the eternal and still renewed meaning of these conceptions. When but starting on the path of life, every child already instinctively understands the value of decoration and knowledge. Only later, under the grimace of disfigured life, does this light of the spirit becomes darkened; while in the kingdom of vulgarity, it has no place and is unknown. Yes, the spirit of the age attains even to such monstrosity!

It is not the first time that I have knocked at these gates, and I here again appeal to you: Among horrors, in the midst of the struggles and the conflicts of the people, the questions of knowledge and art are matters of first importance. Do not be astonished. This is not an exaggeration; neither is it a platitude. It is a decided affirmation.

The question of the relativity of human knowledge has always been much argued. But now, when the whole of mankind has felt, directly or indirectly, the horrors of war, this question has become a vital one. People have not only become accustomed to think but even to speak without shame about things of which they evidently have not the slightest knowledge. On every hand, men repeat opinions that are altogether unfounded. And such judgments bring great harm into the world, an irreparable harm.

We must admit that during the last few years, European culture has been shaken to its very foundation. In the pursuit of things, the achievement of which has not yet been destined to mankind, the fundamental steps of ascent have been destroyed. Humanity has tried to lay hold of treasures that it has not deserved and thus has rent the benevolent veil of the Goddess of Happiness.

Of course, what mankind has not yet attained, it is destined to attain in due time; but how much will man have to suffer to atone for the destruction of the forbidden gates! With what labor and self-denial shall we have to build up the new foundations of culture!

The knowledge that is locked up in libraries or the brains of the teachers again penetrates but little into contemporary life. Again, it fails to give birth to active creative work.

Modern life is filled with the animal demands of the body. We come near to the edge of the terrible magic circle, and the only way of conjuring its dark guardians and escaping from it is through the talisman of true knowledge and beauty.

The time when this will be a necessity is at hand.

Without any false shame, without the contortions of

savages, let us confess that we have come very near to barbarism. Confession is already a step toward progress.

It matters not that we still wear European clothes and, following our habit, pronounce special words. But the clothes cover savage impulses, and the meaning of the words pronounced—although they are often great, touching, and uniting—is now obscured. The guidance of knowledge is lost. People have become accustomed to darkness.

More knowledge! More art! There are not enough of these foundations in life, which alone can lead us to the golden age of unity.

The more we know, the more clearly we see our ignorance. But if we know nothing at all, then we cannot even know we are ignorant. And that being so, we have no means of advancement, nothing to strive for, and the dark reign of vulgarity is inevitable. The young generations are not prepared to look boldly, with a bright smile, on the blinding radiance of Knowledge and Beauty. From where, then, is the knowledge of the reality of things to come? How, then, are wise mutual relations to arise? From where is unity to come—that unity that is the true guarantee of steady forward movement? Only on the bases of true beauty and true knowledge can a sincere understanding between the nations be achieved. The real guide would be the universal language of knowledge and the beauty of art. Only these guides can establish the kindly outlook that is so necessary for future creative work.

The path of animosity, roughness, and abuse will lead us nowhere. Along that way nothing can be built. Does not a soul, does not a conscience still remain in human nature? The real being in man still seeks to attain justice.

Away with darkness—let us do away with malice and

treachery. Mankind has already felt enough of the hand of darkness.

Let me tell you, and remind you, these are not platitudes, not mere words. I give voice to the convinced seeking of the coworker; the only bases of life are Art and Knowledge.

It is just in these hard days of labor, in this time of suffering, that we must steadily recall these kindly guides. And in our hours of trial, let us affirm them with all the power of our spirit.

You say, "Life is hard. How can we think of knowledge and beauty if we have nothing to live on?" or "We are far away from knowledge and art. We have important business to attend to first."

But I say, "You are right, but you are also wrong." Knowledge and art are not luxuries. Knowledge and art are not idleness. It is time to remember this: they are prayer and the work of the spirit. Do you really think that people pray only when overfed or after excessive drinking, or during the time of careless idleness?

No, men pray in the moments of greatest difficulty. So, too, is this prayer of the spirit most needful when one's whole being is shaken and in want of support and when it seeks for a wise solution. Wherein lies the stronger support? What will make the spirit shine more brightly?

We do not feel hunger or starvation; we do not shiver because of the cold. We tremble because of the vacillation of our spirit, because of distrust, because of unfounded expectations.

Let us remember how often, when working, we have forgotten about food, have left unnoticed the wind, the cold, and the heat. Our intent spirit wrapped us in an impenetrable veil.

"The weapon divideth it not, the fire burneth it not, the water corrupteth it not, the wind drieth it not away;

for it is indivisible, inconsumable, incorruptible and is not to be dried away; it is eternal, universal, permanent, and immovable. . . . Some regard the indwelling spirit as a wonder, while some speak and others hear of it with astonishment; but no one realizes it, although he may have heard it described." (Bhagavad Gita, Ch. II)[*]

Of what does the great wisdom of all ages and all nations speak? It speaks of the human spirit. Penetrate in thought into the deep significance of these words and the meaning of your life. You know not the limits to the power of the spirit. You do not know over what impassable obstacles your spirit bears you, but someday you will awaken, unharmed and everlastingly regenerated. And when life is hard and weary, and there seems to be no way out, do you not feel that some helper—your own divine spirit—is speeding to your aid? But his path is long, and your faintheartedness is swift. Yet does the helper come, bringing you both the "sword of courage" and the "smile of daring." We have heard of a family that, in despair, put an end to their lives with fumes of charcoal. Now this was intolerably fainthearted. When the coming victory of the spirit arrives, will not they who have fled without orders suffer fearfully because they did not apply their labor as they should have applied it? It matters not what labor. The drowning man fights against the flood by all possible means. If his spirit is strong, then the strength of his body will increase without measure.

But by what means will you call forth your spirit? By what means will you lay bare that which in man is buried under the fragments of his everyday life? Again and again, I repeat: by the beauty of art, by the depth of

---

[*]   *The Bhagavad Gita, The Book of Devotion: Dialogue Between Krishna, Lord of Devotion, and Arjuna, Prince of India.* William Q. Judge (Translator). 10th ed. (Los Angeles, California: United Lodge of Theosophists, 1920) p. 13.

knowledge. In them, and them alone, are contained the victorious invocations of the spirit. The purified spirit will show you what knowledge is true, what art is real. I am assured that you will be able to call your spirit to your aid. That spirit, your guide, will show you the best paths. It will lead you to joy and victory. But even to victory, it will lead you by a lofty path whose steps are bound together by knowledge and beauty alone—an arduous trial awaits the whole world, the trial by assimilation of truth. After the medieval trials by fire, water, and iron, now comes the trial by assimilation of truth. But if the power of the spirit upheld men against fire and iron, then will that same power raise them up the steps of knowledge and beauty. But this test is more severe than the trials of antiquity. Prepare to achieve! Prepare for that achievement that is a matter of daily life. Meanwhile, have care for everything that serves to advance the perception of truth. Approach with special gratitude all that shows forth the stages of beauty. At this time, all this is especially difficult.

For us Russians, besides the knowledge pertaining to the whole world, stand apart our own Russian art and Russian learning. For us, this universal language of the soul is of infinite importance. It is with special care and tenderness that we should speak the names of those who realize in life that of which we are justly proud.

There are many serious questions before us, but among them, the question of the true culture of the spirit will be the cornerstone.

What can replace this spiritual culture? Food and industry are but the body and the digestion. But it is enough for men to reach out temporarily to the body and the digestion while the spiritual life starves. The spiritual level of the nations has sunk. In the face of all that has happened, in the face of the threatening, indubitable return to savagery, any further sinking of the level will be fatal. In the whole history of mankind, neither food, nor industry, nor intellect unenlightened by the spirit has ever built up true culture. It is with special care that we should treat everything that yet may raise the level of the spirit. I am not dreaming but asserting.

In every process of reconstruction, the level of education and beauty should be raised; in no case should it be forgotten even for a moment. This is not an abstract judgment; on the contrary, it is the task before us.

A great period of reconstruction awaits humanity. You of the new generation—apart from all your daily needs—prepare for the achievement of true, joyous labor.

In Sweden, I said: "We know that Russia has not ceased to be a great country; after enlightened reconstruction on popular principles, it will assume a fit place in the sphere of culture based on its spiritual and natural wealth. We know how incomprehensibly uninformed the West is concerning Russia—even the best of its people. We know with what injurious incorrectness they judge Russian possibilities. But while respecting all the cultural attainments of the East and the West, we feel that we too can justly set forth truly universal treasures, and, in them, express the cultural physiognomy of the great Russian people. For the language of art and knowledge is the only true and international language— the only language of a firmly established public life. In our internal reconstructions, we must, under the benevolent standard of enlightenment, indefatigably introduce beauty and knowledge among the broad masses of people. We must introduce them firmly and actively, remembering that what now lies before is not ideology, not the work of formulating but the work itself—creation; the essence of which is clear and comprehensible without saying many words about it. Not words but deeds! We must remember that the Image of Beauty and

Knowledge will heal the people of slackness of thought and will inspire them with the bases of personal and public resources. It will make plain the essence of work and show the people, in a more comprehensible light, the path to the lofty attainments of the spirit.

"But to attain to these simple, basic forms of assimilation, the Russian intelligentsia, despite the smallness of its numbers, must show self-sacrificingly, mutual goodwill, union, and respect toward the manifold ways of spiritual searching.

"The intelligentsia must spiritually guard itself against the vulgarity and savagery surrounding it. Out of the fragments and the precious stones lovingly discovered, it must build up the Kremlin of great freedom, lofty beauty, and spiritual knowledge."

Again, we know that the material side of life has treacherously seized on mankind, but we do not conceal the fact that the intelligentsia must seek out the path of achievement.

And here, in London, it has already been said:

"We must, by all means, seek to proclaim and widely realize in life the tasks of true art and knowledge, remembering that Art and Knowledge are the best international language, remembering that the strength of a people lies in its spiritual might, which is reinforced from sources of living water. Recollect the wise, popular tale 'The Spring of Dead Water,' i.e., all that exists only for the body caused the limbs of the body to be broken in pieces, but the body could only be brought to life again when sprinkled from the spring of living water. Those sacred springs must be laid open for the healing of Russia. There are no lookers-on; there are only workers."

We have to speak in plain, clear language as if we were in the open street. Now life is filled with the old banners of political parties, worn out like defaced, useless coins. Now life is filled with innumerable, conventional names. Now man is forgotten. Human words are plain and clear, but yet plainer and clearer is the universal language of creative effort with all its mysterious conviction.

The young generation has before it the task of bringing art and knowledge into life. Art and knowledge have often existed in lifelike, locked libraries as pictures turned with their faces to the wall. But the generation of the young must approach this task actively, vitally, in an ideal way, and their work—the simplest everyday work—must be illuminated by searching and victories. The paths of art in their agelong stratification lie so deep and are so innumerable, and the sources of knowledge are so bottomless! What a life of joyous labor lies before you—you who are beginning to work!

Beauty and Wisdom! It is the prayer of the spirit that will raise the countries to the level of majesty. And you, young men and women, can demand the opening of these paths by all means. That is your sacred right. But for the realization of this right, you yourselves must learn to open your eyes and ears and to distinguish truth from lies. Remember clearly, what is needed is not ideology but effectual effort.

Iron rusts. Even steel is eaten away and crumbles if not vitally renewed. So does the human brain ossify if not allowed to perfect itself indefatigably. Therefore, learn to draw near to art and knowledge. These paths are easy later but difficult in the beginning. Surmount them! And you, young people, have before you one of the most wondrous tasks: to raise the bases of the culture of the spirit and to replace mechanical civilization by the culture of the spirit. Of course, you are witnesses of the cosmic process of the destruction of the mechanical civilization and the creation of the foundations of the culture of the spirit. Among national movements, the first place will belong to the revaluation of work, the crown of which is as widely understood as creation and knowledge. Moreover, only these two motive powers make up that international language of which feverishly seeking mankind stands in such need. Creation is the pure prayer of the spirit. Art is the heart of the people. Knowledge is the brain of the people. Only through the heart and through wisdom can mankind arrive in union and mutual understanding. Now to understand is to forgive. The new governments will inscribe on their banners, "The prayer of the spirit, art, and knowledge," and will understand that he who bears with him the true spirit of the national life must not, even for a moment, forget the achievement of spiritual life. Otherwise, the builder will have no path before him, and ruin will await him.

You, the young generation, have the right to demand from the governments the opening of the paths of art and knowledge. You must be able to say with a clear conscience that even when circumstances were hardest, you did not forget those great foundations of life—Beauty and Wisdom; you not only remembered them but, according to your powers, you realized this achievement in your lives, which replaces the joy of destruction with the true joy of creation. In the consciousness of this lies the guarantee of a brighter future for you. You know that outside of art, religion is inaccessible; outside of art, the spirit of nationality is far away; outside of art, science is dark.

You also know that the achievement of the life of the spirit is not the privilege of hermits and anchorites alone. It may be achieved here, in our midst, in the name of that which is most sacred and nearest to the Great Spirit. And the consciousness of the achievement of life will open up to you new and daily possibilities of creation.

So now I speak to you of the young generation about art and knowledge. I know that you, the knights of the people, the knights of the spirit, will not remain in the city of the dead; you will build up a country that will be bright and most beautiful and full of wisdom. Every word should end not in destruction but in upbuilding. We know how mighty creative thought is. So now, in the presence of great searching, we must speak words that proceed from the best sources, "Put aside all prejudices; think freely!" All that is thought in the name of Beauty and Wisdom will be beautiful.

Again, I will say unto you, remember that the time has now come for harmonizing the centers. This condition will be of the first importance in the conflict with "mechanical civilization," which sometimes is erroneously called culture. The spirit buried under the petty details of everyday life and barbarously ground down is already raising its head. Its wings are growing. O, my young friends! Preserve your bright enthusiasm and your eye of goodness.

There is no other way, O friends now scattered! May my call penetrate to you. Let us join ourselves by the invisible threads of the spirit. I turn to you; I call to you in the name of Beauty and Wisdom; let us combine for struggle and work.

ART AND WORLD CULTURE

[*World Unity Magazine.* New York, No. 9, 1929, pp. 1-12]

AS a prayer, we repeat that Knowledge and Beauty are the real cornerstones of evolution—the Gates to a World Community. We affirm this not only as a prayer but even as a command to all humanity. We know that in these spheres all hearts must be united. Love, labor, and noble action are not abstract, misty symbols for the enlightened workers in the beautiful fields of creation. Endlessly, we must repeat this command of Beauty and Knowledge. We must insist that the creative sense of the beautiful should be applied in everyday life, that every household should be beautified, and that the books should have a place of honor in each home.

Many encouraging signs now manifest themselves simultaneously in all countries. Countless hearts scattered over the world consider art, beauty, and knowledge as the most unifying powers. I myself have seen these—our numberless friends. In twenty-five countries, I have witnessed how these vigilant hearts not only rejoiced in Beauty but felt that here lies the one stronghold where their hopes for evolution could be exalted. I have witnessed how, through the application of the Beautiful, they solved so many social and domestic problems. Truly, it is cause for the greatest enthusiasm to perceive how so many different people in many countries consider beauty and knowledge as the great motive power, which set the stones for the coming progress.

We have the right to regard beauty as a real motive

force. For a moment, imagine the history of humanity without the treasures of beauty. For a moment, let us erase from our memories the majestic images of Assyria and Babylon, the dynamic symmetry of Egyptian art. Let us forget the beauty of the Gothic primitives, the enchantment of Buddhist glory, and classic Greece. Let us disrobe the tales of heroes and rulers of the garb of beauty. Without the adornments of beauty, how crude remain the pages of history! Truly, not a single heroic achievement, not one constructive victory, may be imagined without the sense of the beautiful. In creative enthusiasm, the young generation attains the beautiful. How else could illumined enthusiasm enter into our lives? Verily, only from the creative fields of art where are expressed all spheres of the Supreme.

Studying the past, we may affirm that creative art has been the motive power for the progress of life. The form of life is the synthesis of evolution. Is it not an inspiring thought to realize that the evolution of humanity culminates in Beauty?

Verily, we can evaluate art and beauty as the great motive powers in the new conception of life and in the service to humanity for the construction of the approaching and beautiful evolution. In this justified enthusiasm, we can proclaim beauty as a real motive power.

The history of humanity provides splendid evidence of how the creative thought of beauty was evaluated in ancient times.

From former days, perhaps the fifteenth century in Russia, there has come down to us a legend in which Christ is proclaimed as the highest Guardian of Beauty. According to this legend, when Christ was ascending to Heaven, some troubadours approached Him and asked, "Lord Christ, to whom are you leaving us? How can we exist without you?" And Christ answered,

"My children, I shall give you the golden mountains, silver rivers, and beautiful gardens, and you shall be nourished and happy." But, then, St. John approached Christ and said, "Oh Lord, give them not golden mountains and silver rivers. They do not know how to guard them, and someone rich and powerful will attack them and take away the golden mountains. Give them only your name and your beautiful songs, and give the command that all those who appreciate the songs and who care for and guard the singers shall find the gates open to Paradise." And Christ replied, "Yes, I shall give them not golden mountains but My songs, and all who appreciate them shall find the Gates open to Paradise."

Herein you have the essential and vital combination of the World Brotherhood through Beauty, and you see that the highest symbol of human understanding becomes the highest Guardian of Beauty.

Again, we have a quotation from the oldest Russian historical chronicles by the Monk Nestor. These indicate how Prince Jaroslav appreciated knowledge and beauty: "Jaroslav founded Kiev the Great and its Golden Gates with it. Loving the laws of beauty and church, and being a master in books, he read them by day and by night and wrote them, too, thus sowing literary seeds in the hearts of true men that we now reap. But books and images are rivers that carry wisdom through the world and are as deep as rivers. Also, Jaroslav lovingly beautified the churches with images and with splendid gold and silver vessels, and his heart rejoiced upon it."

Besides, we also have beautiful quotations from some later chronicles of the fifteenth and sixteenth centuries, teaching us that the best spiritual achievement for the rulers is to guard art and even to use art in their own life.

Knowing these quotations, one is not surprised to see in the opera *Snegurochka* that the Tsar is, at the same time, an artist and beautifying his own palace. This is not merely a sophisticated message for royalty but also a fundamental reverence for the beauty of the people. For if you ask me what countersign and certificate you would have to show to be allowed to enter a strange village, I would give you the best advice. Enter the village singing, and the more pleasing your song the better your welcome. If they ask you for a certificate, show them a drawing or a painting; it is the certificate best understood, and you will be assured that you can remain there forever. You have your shield and your guard.

Beauty is, in reality, a panhuman feeling existing both in the city and in the wilderness. Often the heart, nourished upon the beauties from the source of Nature, is more open and speaks more vividly the miracle-making, panhuman language.

This we found also in Asia. With real joy, we recollect how everywhere there are the most beautiful traditions that are dedicated to the meaning of creative art. These traditions are vital because in every country of Asia, they regard and speak about works of art in the most beautiful way—using the most refined symbols—so that very often we have to learn these refined expressions dedicated to the beautiful. Let us recollect how the simple Mongol speaks of the perfection of art in the following legend:

In olden times in Kucha, there lived a celebrated painter. Once, as a deposit against a loan, he brought to a merchant his painting representing a head of cabbage and a butterfly and asked for three thousand *sar*. A boy, who was taking the place of the owner of the shop, gave him the requested loan. The owner returned. He was indignant that, for a cabbage and a butterfly, the boy lent so much money. He chased away the boy and considered the money lost. Winter came, and on the appointed day, the artist brought the money and asked to have the painting returned. They took out the painting, and the owner, to his terror, saw that the butterfly had disappeared from the painting. The artist demanded his complete picture as described. The owner was upset. The painter said, "So, you have unjustly thrown out the boy, but now only he can help you." The owner called the boy. For three days, the boy kept the picture near the fire, and the butterfly appeared again. Then the boy said, "You have not appreciated the artist, but he is so perfect that his colors have all the qualities of nature. The butterflies appear in the warm summertime. For the winter they disappear. The same happens also in the painting." Only the warmth of the fire recalled the butterfly to life in winter as well. So perfect is this painter! The owner was ashamed, adopted the boy, and made him rich for his wisdom.

The same simple Mongol repeats what the Buddha said in the Sutras: "The greatest crime is ignorance."

And let us again recollect all those beautiful legends and stories from the *Tao* and the Buddhist world that connect the meaning of art and knowledge with supreme feelings. What beautiful lines the *Tao* dedicated to the true scientists!

During the five years of travel in Asia, we have seen innumerable libraries in each monastery. In every temple, in every ruined Chinese watchtower, there was a library with a collection of most remarkable books—a collection of famous biographies, dictionaries, and books of history and science.

When you see a lonely traveler in the mountains, you may be sure that in his knapsack is a book and a work of art. You may deprive him of everything, and he will resign it, but he will defend his real treasure—the book or the work of art.

* * *

Our motto always was: Humanity is facing the coming events of cosmic greatness. Humanity already realizes that all occurrences are not accidental. The time for the construction of future culture is at hand. Before our eyes, the revaluation of values is being witnessed. Amid the ruins of valueless banknotes, mankind has found the real value of the world's significance. The values of great art are victoriously traversing all storms of earthly commotions. Even the *earthly* people already understand the vital importance of active beauty. And when we proclaim Love, Beauty, and Action, we know, verily, that we pronounce the formula of the international language. This formula, which now belongs to the museum and the stage, must enter everyday life. The Sign of Beauty will open all Sacred Gates. Beneath the Sign of Beauty we walk joyfully. With Beauty we conquer. Through Beauty we pray. In Beauty we are united. And now we affirm these words—not on the snowy heights but amid the turmoil of the city—and realizing the path of true reality, we greet the future with a happy smile.

Now you see that this is not an idealist's dream but for the real construction of practical life. Those who are not blind must see that the question of art now becomes not a technical matter, but everyone acknowledges that the questions of Beauty and creative knowledge have become the most vital factors of life. Formerly, one heard stories of artists dying of hunger while rich financiers built their palaces. Today, events have brought out the reverse; I have heard stories of bankers dying on top of mountains of worthless banknotes. And we have already heard how an entire country could be supported by the price of old tapestries. So, you see how practically this great evolution is working before our eyes. Besides this, another question of the same deep significance is coming into life. Some days ago, a prominent architect told me that he regrets very much not having the constant cooperation of painters and sculptors from the beginning of a project because only through essential collaboration from the very beginning can something really harmonious result. I have often heard dancers say they needed to know something of sculpture and plastic; and, certainly, you have often heard that painters require music and that music evokes the significance of color.

In unifying the institutions, we had significant experience in this direction; showing how necessary it is to combine under one roof the idea that the unity of arts is also not apart from life, and how all musicians, painters, sculptors, architects, and dramatists can be united and supported by each other. Different branches of art do not distract but evoke some new center of the brain not yet utilized. And, certainly, we know that the function of many centers of the brain is still unknown to us.

The Gates of Paradise mentioned in the old legend are not only imaginary. Truly, especially now, we face the most significant time when the vital medium of art is entering home life. Humanity, distressed by political unrest and surrounded by the debris of its old beliefs, is seeing how easily this new emotion, constructive and vital, may be found in daily life.

We have often mentioned that even prisons must be beautified. This is not an allegory. The great prison of life is so easily beautified, and a real key to happiness and joy is to be found therein—the countersign of song and the certificate of creative work!

Finally, if we have witnessed the beautiful evolution of civilization and culture, we may, in the same way, understand what a far more beautiful evolution awaits us. It is near. It is vital. It is practical for everyone.

Should someone ask why, in the melee of our days, one may be concerned with questions of Beauty, you may safely answer, "I know the way of the future." Friends, if we realize how vital Beauty was during ancient times, what immense uses of the emanations of Beauty we can make in our everyday life. If in the Middle Ages Beauty was considered as the "Gates of Paradise," and if even a modest old chronicler of the eleventh century could assert his joy before Beauty, how necessary it is for us to take all practical advantage of this basis of life, and fully fortified by our contemporary discoveries to repeat: "Love, Beauty, Action!"

How all-embracing is Love; how profoundly must be felt the sense of Beauty, and how vitally must we understand the meaning of that virile expression, Action! This command must not be forgotten once we can introduce it into our daily life. The New Era is not far off, and not a single day may be lost. Perhaps you will ask me why we must repeat constantly this prayer of Love and Beauty. Because, frankly, so many avoid Beauty in their everyday life and erroneously seek a reason for this irreparable mistake. If Beauty is the Shield of the World, if the coming evolution is luminously radiant with discovered rays and energies, even the smallest seeds of this splendor must be reflected in our life. The awaiting ones, the aspiring ones, must be the first to prepare the place of Beauty in life. Thus, incessantly, until we see the results, we must repeat this prayer of Beauty—the crown of Action and Love. Beautiful are the necessities and responsibilities of our lives.

We have always said: "The main thing is to collect and safeguard all the flowers of beauty. With the years, you may change your tasks and find some more suited to your taste. Do not close your eyes to the beautiful, flowery meadows of art, and you will carry everywhere the enthusiasm and love for the achievements of far-off, and perhaps anonymous, creators."

Affirming that the Treasures of art and knowledge are the most important Impulses in the growth of humanity; we must surround those milestones of mankind with vibrating love. Such is the task of the collector.

The names of many collectors are recorded in history as inseparable from the creators because in collecting these men themselves became creators. In emphasizing the significance of collecting, we speak of something not abstract but of something vital—something that gives living impetus to the beautiful. This broadened consciousness will lay the best foundations for a truly creative spirit in the new generation.

Collectors, as the antithesis of destroyers, form a special legion beyond epochs and nationalities. By no means are they retrogrades imprisoned in their own egotistical desire of acquisition. Every true collector feels it necessary to share with understanding the spirits of his cultural treasures. In every collector has already flowered the seed of selfless joy toward beauty. Collecting becomes the cultural thermometer of each nation, and one may estimate the cultural level of nations by these revealing milestones.

The collector learns to protect the treasures of creative genius entrusted to him by destiny as an honorary guard. He is not a casual visitor of museums who transfers the complete responsibility upon a curator; he himself is the guard of those treasures that are before him and that will radiate their light upon many after him. Absorbed in the life of creations, the collector extracts the true wisdom of his treasures. From the covetous *Fafnir*, he is transformed into a guard who has won the right to possess the *Ring* of Achievement. The process of collecting is something like a dynamo of artistic creative power that directly acts upon the spirit of the collector. Just as *Mime* brought up *Siegfried*, so bliss may be found in art treasures, whatever their circumstances. As in Heaven so on Earth. And there is nothing extraordinary in the fact that artistic creations are rising in price even in this conventional, earthly valuta. During war and revolutions, the monetary values of the beautiful were conclusively revealed. Whole countries, whole cities that could not protect themselves with land or buildings, found the means of their existence in their artistic treasures. This is a fact of great cultural significance.

There was a time when wives prevented their husbands from acquiring real art objects, preferring property with the belief that it was indestructible. They did not count upon earthquakes. To them, a printed banknote was more valuable than a Rembrandt, an El Greco, or a da Vinci. One cannot blame them when one remembers that they simply did not understand the true, unchangeable values. But now the era of womanhood has come, and woman will be the real protector and collector of the beautiful.

It is also very instructive to observe the great variations of collections from the strictly conservative—which presents only one school or even one group—up to individual combinations. At present time, these latter collections represent a special interest. The trained eye of the connoisseur of the beautiful focuses his attention upon the most modern of these manifestations of art but is aware, as well, of the paths and roots of these recent achievements. Such collections cannot remain without giving place to the expressions of the creators, which were the milestones of the forward movement of art. Superbly, instructive instances are coming to the front. Van Gogh and Gauguin are paired with the great innovator El Greco. The latest modernists are hanging on the same wall with Brueghel the Elder. In such coordination, a place is found also for Giorgione, Italian, and Flemish primitives—all those who laid the steps for the victory of art. In such horizons, collections cease to be narrow and dogmatic, but, excluding every possible intolerance, they verily cultivate the broad meadows of mankind for a future artistic harvest.

The records of collecting reveal that these never-to-be-repeated treasures enhance earthly and spiritual values. Happy is the land where the movement of enlightened collecting has begun. There, the human spirit will flower to reveal new evidence of fortune and peace.

* * *

Humanity, in diverse ways, is striving for peace, and everyone, in his own heart, realizes that this constructive work is a true prophecy of the New Era. In view of this, it is certainly incongruous to hear discussions on the comparative desirability of various bullets, or on whether one type of ship is closer to the conceptions of world unity than the cannons of two battleships. Let us, however, consider these discussions as preliminary steps toward the same great peace that will tame the belligerent instincts of humanity by the resplendent and joyous creations of the spirit.

The fact remains, however, that the shells of even one of these cannons can destroy the greatest treasures of art and science as successfully as a whole fleet. We deplore the loss of the Library of Louvain and the unreplaceable loveliness of the Cathedral of Rheims; we remember the beautiful treasures of private collections that perished during the world's misunderstandings. We do not, however, wish to inscribe above them words of enmity; let us simply say, "Destroyed by human error and recreated by human hope." Nevertheless, errors in this or any other form can be repeated, and other precious milestones of human achievement can be destroyed.

Against such errors of ignorance, we should take immediate measures. And even though these may be only preliminary measures of safeguarding, some very successful steps can be taken. No one can deny that the flag of the Red Cross proved to be of immeasurable value and reminded the world of humanitarianism and compassion.

For this reason, a plan for an International Peace Pact, which would protect all treasures of art and science through an International Flag, has been outlined by the Roerich Museum for presentation through America to all foreign governments. The purpose of the project that has been submitted to the State Department and the Committee on Foreign Relations, is to prevent the repetition of the disasters of the last war on cathedrals, museums, libraries, and other lasting memorials of the creation of the past.

It is the plan of the project to create a flag that will be respected as the International Neutral Territory; this to be raised above museums, cathedrals, universities, and any other cultural center. The plan projected by the Roerich Museum was drawn up according to the codes of International Law by Dr. George Chklaver of the Paris University—lecturer in the Institute of International High Studies—in consultation with Professor Albert Geouffre de la Pradelle, a member of the Hague Peace Court, Vice President of the Institute of International Law of Paris, and member of the Faculty of Law and the Sorbonne. Both are Honorary Advisors of the Roerich Museum.

As set forth in Article I of the Pact, "Educational, artistic, scientific institutions, and artistic and scientific missions shall be deemed as neutral, and, as such, shall be protected and respected by belligerents.

"Protection and respect shall be due to the aforesaid institutions, and missions in all places are subject to the sovereignty of the High Contracting Parties without any discrimination as to the state allegiance of any particular institution or mission."

When the idea of an international cultural flag was

first propounded, we were not surprised to find that it met with unanimous interest and enthusiasm. Experienced statesmen wondered why it had not been thought of before. When we asked our honorary advisors, Dr. George Chklaver and Professor Albert Geouffre de la Pradelle, to frame this idea into an international formula, we received not only a splendidly formulated project of an international agreement but also many answers full of panhuman sympathy. This international flag for the protection of beauty and science would not in any way demean any interests or lead to misunderstandings. On the contrary, it elevates the universal consciousness that must be awakened. As the Red Cross flag needs no explanation to even the most uncultured mind, so does this new flag, guardian of cultural treasures, speak for itself. It is simple enough to explain, even to a barbarian, the importance of safeguarding art and science.

It is imperative to take immediate measures to preserve the noble heritage of our past for a glorious posterity. This can only come if all countries pledge themselves to protect the creations of culture, which, after all, belong to no one nation but the world. In this way, we may create the next vital step for a universal culture and peace.

For the individual, what is the way for the immediate application of beauty? First of all, let us beautify our homes with the sincerest expressions of beauty. As we repeat, perhaps these expressions will be fragmentary, or they will be only fine reproductions of great creations. It does not matter; for even in small fragments of good reproductions, great conceptions are reflected and can lead us to a great understanding.

The sense of the Beautiful purifies our thoughts; nothing may be a greater stimulus for pure thoughts than this self-sacrificing enthusiasm. And finally, once and for all, we must realize that thought, not deed, is the strongest force. And for this reason, the conception of pure thinking is the most practical one. We are not afraid even to use the word practical because we must be constructive, using all material—matter as well as spirit. In this way, we can understand that even these two conceptions are one.

In this great understanding, we may forget all pettiness; and without any sense of destruction, we may beautify and build up the unfinished Towers of Beauty. And in this way, little by little, we will become accustomed to the great sense of Infinity. And to the eternal Great Beginning—the beginning of light, the beginning of enlightenment, the beginning of labor and beautification—that will transform our everyday life, so isolated and timorous, into constant attainment. Thus, transforming the limited "I" into the unconquerable "We."

PEACE TO ALL THE WORLD!
LIFE TO ALL BEINGS!

[*The American Buddhist.* Vol. I, No. 1, January–April, 1930, p. 3]

FORESEEING the future, Lord Buddha said: "The Teaching is like a flame of the torch that lights up numerous fires; these may be used to prepare food or dispel darkness. But the flame of the torch remains unchangingly aglow." (Sutra 42).

In the East are now being erected great Images of Maitreya as a symbol of the approach of the New Era; we understand how much purification and resurrection must be achieved without delay. The knowing one can repeat the words of the sermon: "Let the light be firm as adamant, victorious as the banner of the Teacher, powerful as an eagle, and let it endure eternally."

VIGNETTES OF INDIA

[*Prabuddha Bharata*. Calcutta, Vol. XXXV, No. 10,
October, 1930, pp. 487–490]

IS it really India? A thin shoreline. Meager little trees.
Crevices of desiccated soil. So does India hide its face
from the South.

* * *

Multicolored is Madura with the remains of Dravid-
ian strata. All the life, all the nerve of the exchange,
was near the temple. In the passages of the temple are
the bazaar, the court, the sermon, the reciter of the
Ramayana, the gossip, the sacred elephant who wanders
in freedom, and the camels of the religious processions.
The ingenious stone carving of the temple is colored
with the present-day, crude colors.

Sarma the artist sorrows over it. But the city council
did not listen to him and colored the temple according
to their own plan. Sarma is saddened that so much fine
understanding is gone and has, as yet, been replaced
only by indifference. . . .

Sarma inquires about the condition of artists in
Europe and America. He is genuinely surprised that
the artists of Europe and America can live by the labor
of their hands. It is incomprehensible to him that art
can provide a means of livelihood. With them, the occu-
pation of an artist is the most profitless one. There are
almost no collectors. Sarma himself, tall in white garments with sad, calm speech, awaits something better
and knows all the burden of the present.... Hard is the

life of the Hindu artist. Much resolution is needed in order not to abandon this thorny path. Greetings to the artists of India. Why is it that in all countries of the world, the condition of scientists and artists is so precarious?

* * *

Thorny also is the way of Hindu scientists. Here before us is an example of a struggling, young scientist—a biologist and a pupil of Sir Jagadis Bose. He began his laboratory in the name of Vivekananda. In his peaceful little house above the laboratory is a room dedicated to the relics of Ramakrishna, Vivekananda, and other teachers of this group. This young man, a pupil of the closest pupil of Vivekananda, carries into life the principles of this master who fearlessly proclaimed his evocation to action and knowledge. In this little upper or highest chamber, he formulates his thoughts surrounded by the things that belonged to his beloved leaders. One remembers vividly the portraits of Ramakrishna and his wife. Both faces impress one with their purity and striving. We sat in complete silence near this memorial hearth. Greetings!

* * *

Who can explain why the path of knowledge and beauty is the most difficult? Why does humanity accept with such hesitation all that is predestined? It is, therefore, the greater joy to see in India the signs of an ascent of knowledge and art. It is joyful to see that in India the number of schools is increasing and that legions of new enlightened workers for science and beauty are ready to serve in the victory of evolution.

* * *

In Calcutta, not far behind the city, are two monuments to Ramakrishna. On the shore, Dakshineswar

Temple is where long lived Ramakrishna. Almost opposite, across the river, is the Mission of Ramakrishna—the mausoleum of the Teacher himself, his wife, Vivekananda, and a collection of many memorable objects. Vivekananda dreamed that here at the mausoleum should be a real Hindu University. Vivekananda took care of this place. There is great peace here, and it is with difficulty one realizes oneself so near to Calcutta with all the terror of its bazaars and confusion.

On the memorable day of Ramakrishna, as many as half a million of his admirers gather.

* * *

On the shores of the Ganges, a gray-bearded man, cupping his palms like a chalice, offers his entire possessions to the rising sun. A woman, quickly telling her rhythms, performs her morning *Pranayama* on the shore. In the evening, she may again be there, sending upon the stream of the sacred river a garland of lights as prayers for the welfare of her children. And these fireflies of the woman's soul, prayer-inspired, travel long upon the dark, watery surface. Beholding these offerings of the Spirit, one can even forget the stout priests of the Golden Temples. We are reminded of other things. We recall those Yogis who send into space their thoughts, thus constructing the coming evolution. These are not the usual priests but active hermits; they are bringing our thought nearer to the energy that will be revealed by scientists in the very near future.

Everywhere there is much incense, rose water, and fragrant sandalwood. Hence, the smoke from the bodies in the Burning Ghats of Benares is not turbid. And in Tibet, also, cremation is used.

* * *

Regard the gentle child games of the Orient, and

listen to the complicated rhythms of the chants and soft music. The profanities of the West are not evident.

* * *

Each day a woman's hand molds the sand at the entrance of the house into a special design. This is the symbol that within the house all is well, and there is neither sickness, death, nor discord. If there is no happiness in the house, then the hand of the woman becomes stilled. A seeming shield of beauty is placed before the house by the hand of the woman at the benevolent hour. And little girls at school early on are being taught a variety of designs for the signs of happiness. An inexplicable beauty lives in this custom of India.

Vivekananda called the women of India to work and to freedom. He also asked the so-called Christians, "If you so love the Teaching of Jesus, why do you not follow it?" So spoke the pupil of Ramakrishna who passed through the substance of all Teachings and learned through life "not to deny." Vivekananda was not merely an industrious *Swami*—something lion-like rang out in his letters. How he is needed now!

* * *

"Buddhism is the most scientific and most cooperative teaching," says the Hindu biologist, Bose. It is a joy to hear how this truly great savant, who found his way to the mysteries of plant life, speaks about the Vedanta, Mahabharata, and the poetry of the legends of the Himalaya. Only true knowledge can find a merited place for all existing things.

Bose's mother, in her day, sold all her jewels to give her son an education. The scientist, in demonstrating his kingdom, says: "Here are the children of the rich in luxurious conditions. See how they become puffed and baggy. They need a good storm to bring them back to healthy normalcy." Knowing the pulse of the plant world, the scientist approaches wholesomely all the manifestations of life. One of Bose's best books was written on the heights of Punjab in Mayavati in the shrine of Vivekananda. Vivekananda departed too soon. Bose and Tagore—noble images of India!

* * *

Some of the most cosmogonic parts of the Vedas are written by women, and now in India has arrived the epoch of the woman. Greetings to the women of India!

* * *

Ramakrishna says: "In Atman, there is no distinction of male or female, of Brahmin or Kshatriya, and the like."

Ramakrishna executed the work of the sweeper to show, personally, that there were no distinctions.

* * *

Sir Jagadis Bose affirms that the sensitiveness of plants is completely astonishing. As the plants feel the formation of a cloud long before it is visible to the eye, so the East feels the thought at its inception.

* * *

In the close interrelation between the visible and the invisible, and the epic simplicity of their interplay, lies the charm of India.

* * *

In sudden support of fundamental Buddhism, the realist of realists, Huxley, says, "No one but a superficial thinker rejects the teaching of reincarnation as nonsense. Like the Teaching of evolution itself, reincarnation has its roots in the world of reality and is entitled to the same support commanded by every consideration that evolves from analogies."

* * *

L.Horn writes: "With the acceptance of the Teachings of evolution, the old forms of thought everywhere are crumbling. New ideas arise in the place of outlived dogmas, and we have before us the spectacle of a general intellectual movement in a direction becoming ever more strange—parallel with Eastern philosophy.

"The unheard-of speed and variety of the scientific progress current in the last fifty years, cannot but call forth an equally unprecedented hastening of thought in the broad non-scientific circles of society. That the highest and most complete organisms develop out of the simplest organisms; that upon one physical basis of life stands the whole living world; that there cannot be traced a line that divides animal and vegetable kingdoms; that the difference between life and non-life is a difference in gradation and not substance—all this already has become commonplace in the new philosophy. After the recognition of physical evolution, it is not difficult to say that the acknowledgment of psychic evolution is only a question of time."

The observation of the East astonishes and rejoices one—not the obvious power of observation that leads to a dead stereotype but observation fine and silent in its substance. One remembers how the teacher asked the newly arriving pupil to describe a room, but the room was empty, and in a vessel was swimming only a tiny fish. In three hours, the pupil wrote three pages, but the teacher rejected him saying that about this one little fish he could have written all his life. In technical imitation is revealed the same sharp observation. In the adaptation of the meter of a song, in the character of a call, in movements, you see an all-powerful culture. Somewhere, the Hindus enveloped in their mantles were compared to Roman senators. This is an inane comparison. Rather liken them to the philosophers of Greece and, still better, call them the creators of the Upanishads, Bhagavad Gita, and Mahabharata. For neither Rome nor Greece existed when India was flourishing. The latest excavations begin to support this indubitable deduction.

* * *

Hindus regard objects of art with fine understanding. From a Hindu, you naturally expect an interesting approach and unusual remarks, and so it is. Therefore, to show paintings to a Hindu is a real joy. How captivatingly they approach art! Do not think that they are occupied only in its contemplation. You will be astonished by their remarks about tonality, technique, and the expressiveness of the line. If the observer is long silent, do not think that he has become tired. On the contrary, this is a good sign. It means he has entered a mood, and one can expect from him especially interesting deductions. Sometimes, he will tell you a whole parable, and there will be nothing vulgar or crude about it. It is astonishing how transformed are the people of the East before the creations of art. Indeed, it is more difficult for a European to enter the current of creation, and, as a rule, he is less able to synthesize his impression.

* * *

India, I know your sorrows, but I will remember you with the same joyous tremor as the first flower in the spring meadow. From your Brahmins, we will select the greatest who understood the Vedic Wisdom. We will select the Rajah who strove for the finding of the path of Truth. We will notice Vaishya and Shudra, who have exalted their craft and labor for the upliftment of the world. A boiling kettle is the forge of India. The dagger of faith over a white goat. The phantom flame of a bonfire over a widow. Conjurations and sorcery. Complicated are the folds of your garments, India. Menacing are your vestures blown by the whirlwind. And deadly burning are your inclement rocks, India. But we know your fragrant essences. India, we know the depth and finesse of your thoughts. We know the great AUM, which leads to the inexpressible Heights. We know your great Guiding Spirit, India; we know your ancient wisdom! Your sacred scriptures in which are outlined the past, the present, and the future. And we will remember you with the same tremor as the most precious, first flower in the spring meadow.

INDIA OPEN GATES—AN ADDRESS

[*The Roerich Museum Bulletin.* New York, Vol. I, No. 11,
November, 1931, pp. 3–4]

BEFORE us are five cables[*] pertaining to the Conference in Bruges:

"*Congrès Union Internationale pour Pacte Roerich adresse salut au Maître et fervents souhaits pour réalisation noble idée— Beyaert Secretaire Bruges.*"

"Splendid article appeared Times from Bruges Correspondent Stop All Bruges hailing America in gratitude to you Stop American flag to hang from every Bruges window every Flemish matron sewing American flags."

"Bruges Conference opened with four hundred delegates great pomp mass at Basilica Holy Blood, then procession to bless and crown Roerich Peace Banner with Bruges Coat of Arms Stop Messages received Pope and King Albert endorsing Pact also from ambassadors statesmen ministers United States Senators, educators Stop City Bruges presented Roerich with medal especially struck in his honor as leader world culture and peace Stop Roerich declaration read amid cheers Stop Delegates cities of France Belgium Italy also Governments France Belgium Greece Stop French President's message bestowing the Roerich Grand Cross Legion of Honor hailed with cries *Vive Roerich* Stop All Roerich resolutions accepted; Stop Conference tremendous success Stop Great vision hailed as epochal in world peace."

---

[*]   Telegrams sent following the First Conference in Bruges for the Roerich Pact in 1931. They are left unedited to retain authenticity.—Ed.

"Unitedly we send you congratulations on this great day when Banner of Peace is victoriously proclaiming your great Leadership of Culture—Trustees Roerich Museum."

"Meeting held Museum commemorating Bruges Conference passed resolutions endorsing your epochal plan for peace mailing resolutions to you, also to President United States—President Roerich Museum."

I congratulate the Trustees of the Museum. I congratulate our Honorary Advisers, coworkers, deans, teachers, students, and all our fellow members upon the success of this First Conference in the name of Culture and Peace!

On the thirteenth of September, I wrote from Lahul that the homunculi and the ignorant would still try to obstruct our cultural beginnings. Hypocritically, they would whisper that we admit war and are indifferent to human life. However, they should understand that our Pact and Banner are not only for times of war but have a general cultural significance. Culture naturally brings with itself peace—and peace safeguards the creations of human genius as well as human life. But the ignorant and the other servitors of darkness will, of course, continue their whispering and their efforts to undermine. For every ray of Light is displeasing to them, and every measure toward destruction gives them those particles of decomposition upon which they thrive. The struggle with ignorance is already a spiritual achievement for Light.

It is touching to think that the old Cities of Van Eycks and Mendings so vividly responded to our Pact and impelled it toward a real activity that will remain unforgettable in the history of Culture. What glorious names—national and religious leaders and heads of education—were with us during the days of the Conference! The International Union for our Pact has been declared a permanent Institution. This resolution indeed corresponds to our suggestion to make Bruges the Headquarters of the Union. With the noble environs of the Palace of Peace and Permanent Court of International Justice in the Hague, there may be concentrated all cultural forces, which, realizing clearly the undeferrable need, had decided to unite actively in offering their labors in the name of establishing the traditions of Culture. In this, the members of the International Union respond to the most urgent demand for Culture. They have decided not only to safeguard the past but also to create nobility of striving among the young generation; the milestones of the past should not only bear evidence of the glorious past but should prove the true impulse toward beautiful construction. These noble activities are so undeferrably needed that in mutually greeting each other with the success of the Conference, we do not, thereby, presuppose the victory. But we regard it as the opening of the Gates through which we are to carry—each according to his whole strength—all that is most precious, remembering that the highest desire of humanity is to live in a world of Culture.

The Banner of Culture and Peace, the World Day of Culture, the cataloging of world treasures of human genius, *Oriflamma*—a journal to manifest these creative treasures—cordial meetings, and uninterrupted and enthusiastic exchange of worthy proposals, all of this will afford to our International Union not only vivid activity but also an endless growth of possibilities. We ask all our societies and institutions that are adhering to the Union to unfurl at once the Banner of Culture and Peace; no time must be lost. We must immediately begin the good deed of construction with the unbreakable enthusiasm with which the best pages of the history of humanity have been built.

It is immediately necessary to include in the programs of all our societies and institutions near to us, activities to aid the Union and the Banner. Every society of ours is already a member of the International Union for our Pact and, thus, is already responsible for the flourishing of the idea of Culture, which alone can unite the world in construction for Good. In every country, the ideas of culture will be reflected in different ways. Only broad containment and mutual respect can now help to prevent absurd disunity and disparagement.

Thus, in the name of unity, in the name of brilliant cooperation, in the name of the great world culture, in the name of the foundations of peace, let us unite all our strivings. Let us, in friendly collaboration, achieve that which will bring to the coming generations joy and happiness.

Naggar, September 30, 1931.

IN MEMORIAM

[*The Maha-Bodhi.* Vol. XL, No. 7–9, 1933, pp. 244–246]

WHEN I wrote my last "Message of Friendliness" for the Vaisakha Number of *The Maha Bodhi Journal,* I looked at the portrait of the Venerable Anagarika Dharmapala on the wall before me, and speaking of friendliness as the basic principle of life, I addressed the Venerable Dharmapala—knowing that from him I could expect a response and sympathy in the question of the unification of hearts. Verily, the glorious life of this Messenger of Truth passed under the sign of Friendliness, Enthusiasm, and Unification!

Though several meetings were intended, we never had the opportunity to come together physically, but yet I often met the Venerable Dharmapala in thought. On various continents, I have heard and read his esteemed name, and everywhere the same feeling surrounded it. It was the feeling of noble reverence. Everywhere the best people vouched by him in thought during hours of elevating, inspiring, and deep work.

In our present perturbed times, such a constant veneration is very rare. People always try to involve great names in some outside, unnecessary circumstances, but if they do not dare to use a name in this superficial way, it is always the best sign of their true admiration.

Few are the number of pioneers who have witnessed as many remarkable events as the Venerable Dharmapala, and, therefore, it is especially painful if one of these rare Spirits departs to a better world but away from ours. Of course, such untiringly laboring and continuously creative Souls will never cease their noble endeavors in any world. People with such a clear, devoted consciousness never remain inactive. From one fruitful life, they turn to another achievement, remembering that the Arhat's rest consists of new beautiful thoughts. And, of course, such thoughts will be first of all directed to the Peace of all beings, to self-perfection, and to all preordained noble deeds that bring with them the good for everyone. Was not such non-egotism the dominating side of the character of the Venerable Dharmapala! And does not the constant striving toward constructiveness and creation distinguish him in the field of earthly labors!

When we remember all that he has done, everything in which he participated, and everything with which his name is connected, does it not all form the most glorious wreath of honor, consisting of innumerable flowers that all fluoresce in their innermost Beauty! When we have the possibility at the departure of a great personality to apply the conception of Beauty, it means that our heart is indeed deeply moved. It means that the achievement that was before us has kindled our hearts. And in these sacred fires of the heart, we can unite in best thoughts and know that also the departed, who is entering a new field of labor, nods his head in a benevolent smile.

Hail to the Venerable Messenger of Goodwill!

Hail to the Leader of unselfish Creativeness!

Hail to the Guardian of the Great Teaching!

GREAT MOTHER OF
THE BANNER OF PEACE

[*Peace.* Godavari, Vol. VI, No. 11-12, 1933, pp. 385-386]

A Dedication
*to The Washington Banner of Peace Convention,
November 1933*

SANTI, Santi, Santi!
Great Mother, Thou Golden Flamed One!
Great Mother of the Banner of Peace!
Thou Mother art our Trust! Save Thee
    who will raise this World Banner,
The Sign which guards men's loftiest treasures!
Save Thee, who will hasten in aid
    to unfurl the Banner as Shield of Creation.

Though the seas rage and the gales threaten
Fearlessly, Thou shalt the Banner affirm
    and fill to overflowing all human hearts
    with joy for the Spirit's most sacred treasures.
Thou knowest the peril if the Sign be stayed;
Thou knowest how oft dark destruction cowed the
    earth, how men's most high, most needed
    layed abased.

If the flock know not the peril, Thou Pastoress
    shall raise the Banner, as Peace Invocation.
All mountain winds shall hasten Thy Command:
    to guard, to build, to raise tomorrow's Wonder.

Thy golden flame all darkness shall dispel,
Thy hand erect! Thy breath shall heal all pain,
   and soft caress shall even stones awaken!

The Mighty Triune Symbol raise, oh Mother!
We know to Thee abhorrent is destruction
   and violation of human hearts' abodes.
To Thee repulsive is all chaos and all darkness.
In Peace and in Creation shines Thy Armour.
Thee we implore—do not deny this prayer:
Aid us, Great Mother of Glorious Peace!

TO THE WORLD LEAGUE OF CULTURE

[*Roerich Museum Bulletin.* New York, Vol. III, No. 6,
June, 1933, pp. 1–2]

BEFORE us we have a vast number of periodicals published in India. They are most significant in regard to both their quantity and variety, justly, in keeping with the characteristics of this great continent. We will mention several names outside of the stupendous number of publications in Bengali, Urdu, Tamil, and other Hindu and Moslem dialects.

Here is the voluminous *Kalyan*, devoted to the highest spiritual concept. Here are the publications of the Visva-Bharati, permeated with the noble, enlightened spirit of the great poet of India, Rabindranath Tagore. Here is the *Modern Review*, with its wide response under the experienced guidance of its revered editor, Ramananda Chatterjee. Here is the *Maha Bodhi Journal*, directed by the benevolent hand of the venerable Sri Devamitta Dharmapala, and the *Ceylon Buddhist* of the Y.M.B.A., where P. Siriwardhana works untiringly. Here is an entire series of good journals of the Ramakrishna Mission, such as the *Prabuddha Bharata* in Mayavati, *Vedanta Kesari* (Madras), the *Morning Star* (Patna). Here is the *Scholar* from Palghat, with its wide cultural, artistic, and scientific program. Here is the evocative *Dawn*, saturated with the religious and cultural teachings of the esteemed Sadhu Sri Vaswani. Here is the beautifully edited *Rupam*, of which O. Gangoly can justly be proud.

Here is a legion of periodicals indicating the best

educational aims: *Kalpaka, Educational Review* (Madras), *Young Folk, Upasana, Student, Trivent, Indian Educator, Orient* (Bombay), *Theosophist, Young Builder, All-India Trade Magazine, The Field, The Singalese* (Ceylon), *Current Science, Journal of the Geological Society, Journal of Mining and Metallurgy, The Forester, Indian Science, Literary Review* of D. B. Taraporevala, various organs of the Botanical Survey and the Archaeological Survey, *The Journal of the Bombay Society of Natural History*, publications of the Bose Institute, *The Annual of the Biological Chemists' Society of India, Indian Historical Quarterly, Journal of the Asiatic Society of Bengal*, and *Journal of the Bombay Branch of the Royal Asiatic Society.* . . .

It is impossible to cite in its entirety the complete colorful multitude of equally useful publications that guide cultural thought. The *Indian Yearbook* indicates that there are 5,362 printing presses, 1,378 newspapers, and 3,089 periodicals. During one year, 2,117 books in English and other European languages, and 14,276 books in Hindu, Moslem, and other vernacular tongues were published. Amid the world ocean of the press, such strongholds of thought constitute a beautiful island.

Out of the entire educational asset, even these few mentioned titles already characterize a whole world of philosophic, scientific, and social thought—majestic in its traditions, millenniums-old. In our days of diffusion and perversion, it is precious to witness the depths of existing living thought!

Often people speak of the past and only of the past. And we seem to be ashamed of the present, especially when it concerns philosophic and scientific thinking, which by many of our contemporaries is regarded as something remote, abstract.

At present, too many persons believe that religion, philosophy, culture, science, and the art of thinking are abstract and that to dwell on them, at present, is untimely. Also, the so-called true realities are trade, industry, and accounting.

Therefore, it is such a joy to see not only books devoted to the true values but also monthly and weekly periodicals where the daily thought pulsates in all its incessant, untiring strength. You know how monthly and weekly periodicals require continual kindling and concentrated labor.

Only recently, I wrote to you about friendliness as the adamant of the world. In these manifold editions, one does not notice any malicious polemics. One notices the predominance of facts of research and the profound philosophical approach to questions of vital necessity. Even such an apparently specialized journal as the *All-India Trade Magazine* heads an issue with an article, "The Cultural Mission of the Modern Merchant," and concludes it with a beautiful quotation from Goethe. In this way, the cooperation of commerce and Culture—a relationship that is so often mutilated in the concave prisms of contemporary life—finds a dignified solution.

One immediately notices the absence of vulgar jokes and all the trash attached to the perverted notion of a so-called *good time.*

One also notices that instead of crass intolerance, there can often be found a benevolent treatment of a neighbor's point of view. Certainly, we always select the kindest and best because in the domain of Culture, one can only travel along positive milestones.

The milestones of evil and darkness have already lured humanity into the labyrinths of black magic, from which neither nudism, golf, gambling on the stock exchange, races, nor record-breaking matches can help to find a way out. Where will it lead, this pugilistic speed? A human being may also slip downhill toward the precipice at terrific speed. This would also be an extraordinary speed!

The number of serious articles dedicated to the women's movements, youth, and experimental research also makes one rejoice. Constructiveness and seriousness of exposition also indicate the demands of the reader. And these thousands of publications—in reality, the number is even greater than that given—have their circles of readers. They somehow exist, are regularly issued, and in most cases, probably are published by people who know what work is and who usually are not wealthy.

At a time of general depression, amid all sorts of upheavals, it is truly precious to record the facts of a firm spirit. Let these be multiform; for Culture, as such, has also infinite aspects, yet it still remains One in its radiant, creative foundation.

It is always necessary to look for facts without prejudice and conventional limitations—facts in which the human heart resounds. Our duty is to collect and to record these facts of accumulation of the spirit. Thus are the treasuries of true values erected. In the hours of depression, one may primarily renew one's strength, unbreakable vigor, patience, joyousness, and all the creative principles of life from these true treasures.

It is infinitely inspiring to see with one's own eyes this multitude of serious publications that expand and sensitize the consciousness, and which exist as the best indication that they are needed and welcomed by many millions of hearts.

Please convey to all our societies, institutions, and committees the thought that each of them, in its own country, should collect and present a brief digest and description of the press and publications. Let all our European, Japanese, South American, and South African Societies give such reports; they will constitute a most valuable symposium on the direction of contemporary thought.

Let no one attach too much attention to negative

matters. Every expression, ugliness, and ignorance is contagious and depressing. May all our coworkers proceed by positive, radiant paths. And, as always, let us remember that only the sparks of positive constructiveness kindle hearts and awaken creative joy.

PEACE THROUGH CULTURE

[*Peace*. Godavari, Vol. VI, No. 9, September, 1933, pp. 301–303]

THE whole world will rejoice when hearing that on November 17th this year, in Washington, the Convention for the Banner of Peace will take place for the protection of the treasures of Religion, Art, and Science. The great conception of Peace is pronounced in all religions, in all creeds and faiths. Every human language has this beautiful word. And there is no such stony heart that would not throb in enthusiasm for peaceful endeavors.

Humanity, in diverse ways, is striving for peace, and everyone, in his heart, realizes that this constructive work is a true prophecy of the New Era. In view of this, it is certainly incongruous to hear discussions on the comparative desirability of various bullets, or on whether one type of warship is closer to the conception of world unity than the cannons of two battleships. Let us, however, consider these discussions as preliminary steps toward the same great peace that will tame the belligerent instincts of humanity by the resplendent and joyous creations of the spirit.

The fact remains, however, that the shells of even one of these cannons can destroy the greatest treasures of art and science as successfully as a whole fleet. We deplore the loss of the Library of Louvain and the unreplaceable loveliness of the Cathedral of Rheims; we remember the beautiful treasures of the private collections that perished during the world's misunderstandings. We do not, however, wish to inscribe above them words of enmity; let us simply say: "Destroyed by human error and recreated by human hope." Nevertheless, errors in this or any form can be repeated, and other precious milestones of human achievement can be destroyed.

Against such errors of ignorance, we should take immediate measures. And even though these may be only preliminary measures of safeguarding, some very successful steps can be taken. No one can deny that the flag of the Red Cross proved to be of immeasurable value and reminded the world of humanitarianism and compassion.

At our Peace Pact meeting in 1929, we proposed a special Banner of Peace for the protection of all cultural treasures. Two Committees for promoting the Peace Pact were elected in New York and Paris. An International Union for the Roerich Pact was established with its central seat in Bruges, where already two world Congresses for spreading the ideals of Peace through Culture were in session, resulting in the inauguration of the *Roerich Foundation pro Pace, Arte, Scientiae et Labore.*

From Temples, from shrines of spirituality, from all light-bearing centers, should thunder ceaselessly the worldwide call to eliminate the very possibility of wars and create for generations to come new, lofty traditions of the veneration of real cultural treasures. By unfurling the Banner of Peace everywhere, untiringly, we destroy the very physical field of war.

Let us also affirm the World Day of Culture, when simultaneously in all temples, schools, and educational institutions, the world will be reminded of the true treasures of humanity, of creative heroic enthusiasm, of the betterment and adornment of life. For this purpose, we have not only to safeguard, by all available means, our cultural heritage but we must consciously value these treasures, remembering that every contact with them will already ennoble the human spirit.

As we have already witnessed, wars cannot be stopped by interdicts nor can malice nor falsehood be prohibited. But undeferrably, patiently striving to the highest treasures of humanity, we may make these issues of darkness altogether inadmissible as a progeny of gross ignorance. The ennobled, expanded consciousness, having contacted the Realm of Light, will naturally enter the path of peaceful construction, discarding as shameful rubbish all belittlement of human dignity generated by ignorance.

The lists of adherers to the Banner of Peace are already long and glorious. The Banner has already been consecrated during the Congress in Bruges.

The one panhuman desire to safeguard the achievements of mankind is not so much a new law but the imperative wish, which is so urgently needed. Every endeavor, even the most evident, requires an active start. For Peace and Culture, one does not even need a unanimously world-wide votum. The beautiful principles of the General Good can be affirmed on every scale, still retaining their vital potentiality. Let us greet wholeheartedly all coworkers: "Without delay, proceed victoriously in your full abilities along this glorious Path through Culture toward Peace."

Verily, time is short; lose neither day nor hour! Kindle the flame of the heart with indomitable enthusiasm. Under the Banner of Peace, let us proceed toward the One Supreme Light in powerful union, in the name of the Highest—the Most Beautiful.

BANNER OF PEACE

Washington Convention for Roerich Peace Pact, 1933

[*New Haven Teacher's Journal.* Vol. XXVII, No. 1,
October, 1933, pp. 14–16]

THE whole world ponders about peace. Everyone in his language, within his possibilities, pronounces this great conception that leads humanity to self-perfecting.

It does not matter if everything cannot be done at once. But let space be cemented with this mighty call. May our age bear the seal of peace, creative labor, and true cooperation.

On November 17, the Convention of the Banner of Peace in Washington will discuss the most immediate measures for introducing into life our Banner Protector, which like a watchful guardian should be unfurled over all treasuries of Art and Knowledge. It will wave over monuments of Religions and Culture, calling for the preservation of the real treasures of mankind. May all friends of peace, all friends of the preservation of treasures of human genius be with us on that day!

I am fully convinced that this idea will enter into life. The thought of the protection of cultural treasures of humanity preoccupied me for several decades, and the sad events of life itself strengthened my project still more. Already in 1904, addressing the Society of Architect Artists in St. Petersburg, I outlined this idea, calling attention to the tragic condition of many state architectural monuments. My extensive travels to ancient monasteries and historical cities—also the archaeological excavations in such important places as Novgorod and other regions linked with the most ancient traditions—gave me rich material to affirm the necessity for urgent measures to protect cultural treasures. Later, in 1914, after the destructions, when many irreparable historical monuments perished, I made a similar report to the late Emperor Nicholas II and the late Commander-in-Chief, Grand Duke Nicholas. Both reports met with great sympathy, and only such extraordinary havoc as the war prevented its immediate development. Then, as President of the Exhibition of Allied Nations where Flemish, French, British, and the arts of other allied nations were beautifully represented, I had again a happy opportunity to propound this idea and was convinced that sooner or later the protection of cultural treasures would become a sacred reality in the world.

With new ardor, these thoughts preoccupied me when we had to witness no longer the vandalism of warfare but the vandalism of the time of peace. For an untrained eye, it is quite impossible to imagine how many cultural treasures that can never be replaced are exposed to danger and perish without leaving any traces. One of our foremost duties is to apply all our efforts to direct public attention to their real treasures. Each day brings news of some new destruction. We are already imbued with the idea that precious monuments must not be carried away but must be safeguarded where they stand—more so because the possibilities of modern transportation make even the remotest places accessible. I am deeply convinced that universal attention will be paid to cultural treasures, and, as its symbol, the universally unifying Banner will bring profound and absolute usefulness to the cultural development of the peoples.

I am not astonished that we receive so many enthusiastic responses to our Banner of Peace. The past is filled with deplorably sad and irreparable destruction. We see that not only in times of war but also during other moments of unrest, creations of human genius are destroyed. At the same time, the elite of humanity understands that no evolution is possible without the accumulations of Culture. We understand how indescribably difficult are the ways of Culture; hence, the more carefully must we guard the paths that lead to it. It is our duty to create for the young generation traditions of Culture. Where there is Culture, there is Peace, there is achievement, and there is the right solution for difficult social problems. Culture is the accumulation of the highest Bliss, highest Beauty, and highest Knowledge. In no other way can humanity pride itself on having served sufficiently the florescence of Culture. After a state of ignorance, we reach civilization, then gradually acquire education, then comes intelligence, then follows refinement, and this synthesis opens the gates to high Culture.

We must admit that our precious and unique treasures of Art and Science are not even properly cataloged. And if our Banner of Peace may be the impetus to urge such a result for universal treasures, this alone would be the fulfillment of a colossal task. How much of the useful and beautiful could be easily attained! Let us imagine a universal day of Culture when, simultaneously, all schools of the world will be extolled the true treasures of nations and humanity.

Among the many works of enthusiasm must be pointed out the great sympathy of the Women of America. The representatives of the five million have pledged their support for the Peace Banner. Vast is the list of organizations, societies, libraries, museums, schools, and statesmen, whose members have expressed the great hope that this project will enter into life. Several organizations have already hoisted the Banner of Peace. The Museum Commission of the League of Nations under the presidency of M. Jules Destree, Belgian Minister, has unanimously accepted this project. In 1931, the first special Conference was held at Bruges. Mr. C. Tulpinck, President of the Union International pour le Pacte Roerich, presided; and Dr. Adachi, President of the Permanent Court of International Justice, was Protector of the Conference. In connection with this Conference, the proposed League of Cities united under the same Banner of Peace was of great interest. Our friend, the poet Marc Chesneau, represented the old city of Rouen. Dr. Georges Chklaver's article, "Le Pacte Roerich et la Societe des Nations," highly recommended the Pact from the point of view of the law. Truly, the protection of the treasures of culture belongs to those all-unifying foundations upon which we can gather in friendship without any petty feeling of envy and malice.

On August 9, 1932, the Second Conference in Bruges, in which seventeen countries took part, was convened by the "Union International Pour le Pact Roerich" for the purpose of bringing about the defense of artistic and scientific treasures. The Conference, greeted in the name of His Majesty King Albert of Belgium and by a message from the Belgian Prime Minister, took place amid great enthusiasm and was concluded with a series of projects for introducing our Pact to the whole world. Besides the already existing Union, the City of Bruges placed at the Union's disposal a separate building for the inauguration of the Roerich Foundation for Peace, Art, Science, and Labor. For this museum, many valuable exhibits have been donated. Thus, the city of Paris presented an artistic collection, and several private collectors have also expressed their desire to donate collections to this museum.

Amongst the people who took close participation

in the discussions of the Conference have to be mentioned—the President of the Union, C. Tulpinck; the representative of the city of Paris, Counselor Brunesseauz; the Consul General of France, the Honorable Leon Guermonprez who had been officially delegated to represent the French Government; the Duke of Argyll; the delegate of Great Britain, Mr. Murray; the well-known Professor of International Law, Baron de Taube; the Delegation of the Roerich Institutions headed by the President of the European Center in Paris, Mme. de Vaux Phalipau; the General Secretary, Dr. G. Chklaver; Count de Roenefort; the architect Rey de Villette; the representatives of Czecho-Slovakia, Greece, and seventeen other countries took part in the exhibition and the Conference. The Conference in Bruges was greeted in the name of His Majesty King Albert of Belgium and by a message from the Belgian Prime Minister. Amongst the messages and greetings were highly sympathetic messages from: Marshall Lyautey; the President of the Court of International Justice at the Hague, Dr. Adachi; letters from Dr. Rabindranath Tagore; Sir Jagadis Bose; Professor Sir C. V. Raman; the Principal of the School of Arts and Crafts, Lucknow; A. K. Haidar; the Maha Bodhi Society; Maurice Maeterlinck; Senator Copeland of New York; numerous women's Leagues, scientific organizations, and representatives of the world of Culture. Having taken a series of practical measures for the near future, the Conference closed its session with the firm conviction that our Pact would be established without delay and would find world adoption.

Now in Washington will assemble the friends of Peace. President Roosevelt is open to everything positive and constructive. Mrs. Franklin D. Roosevelt writes about our Pact: "I think the ideals represented by the Roerich Pact cannot help but appeal to all those who hope that the best in the past may be preserved to guide and serve future generations."

A member of the Cabinet, Secretary Henry A. Wallace, in the course of a letter to me writes: "I have for several years been interested in your endeavor to create a community of feeling among all of the nations concerning those things that have to do with the arts and sciences. Your endeavor to furnish a symbol for the thought that beauty and knowledge should tie all the nations together in appreciation of a common human purpose—however separate their apparent paths may be—has been of profound interest to enlightened people over the entire world for several years. It is appropriate that you should have a meeting in Washington next fall to consider the things for which the Banner of Peace stands. I believe so profoundly in the things for which the Banner of Peace stands that I am only too happy to offer you any cooperation, in my personal capacity, to help make your efforts along this line successful."

Amongst the latest expressions of sympathy with the Pact, I cannot omit mentioning the powerful statement of the Italian Ambassador in Washington, Signor A. Rosso, of our delegation. He said: "I feel no one can be against such a great idea. Whoever would go against the Roerich Pact will have the sanctuary of public opinion to deal with."

Verily, humanity is tired of destructions, vandalism, and negation. Positive creativeness is the fundamental quality of the human spirit. In our life, everything that uplifts and ennobles the spirit must hold the dominant place. The milestones of the glorious path must from childhood impel our spirit to the beautiful future. Be assured it is not a truism to speak about the undeferrable and urgent strivings to Culture. If some ignoramus finds this idea superfluous and needless, we will say to him: "Poor ignoramus, you are out of the hands of evolution, but remember that we are a legion; in no way shall we yield in our idea of a Peace Banner. If you are the obstructionist, we shall transform your obstacles into possibilities."

The Washington Convention gathers under the most favorable signs. Let there resound, once again, the mighty prayer for Peace of the entire world. As the Red Cross affirms physical health, so may the Banner of Peace establish and affirm the spiritual health of mankind!

Himalayas, 1933.

BANNER OF PEACE

[*Prabuddha Bharata.* Calcutta, October, 1933, pp. 500–502]

PEACE to all beings! What can be more majestic than the march under the Banner of Peace? What can be more wonderful than the participation in this march under the banner of peaceful labor and creative constructiveness of the hosts of youth, singing hymns of beautiful achievements!

And now this sublime manifestation of great Culture is no longer a dream but is going to become a reality.

Already for the third time, the defenders of Peace and Culture gather for the affirmation of the Banner— Protector of all real treasures of human genius. On November 17, 1933, in Washington are gathering friends of the Banner of Peace. And on the same day in many countries will resound greetings to the Banner. Everywhere there will assemble old and young, and everyone will send, in his own way, thoughts about the peace of the whole world and the unity of human hearts in the name of Light and Culture. At the head of the march of Peace, I visualize the great peace-bearer, the Blessed Bhagavan Sri Ramakrishna, and the Lion of Truth, Swami Vivekananda, who so often in his enlightened messages pointed out the great value of art and science as leading principles of evolution. And, of course, this radiant call always resounded in the hearts that remain forever young.

Is this not a festival! Is not the great Festival of Cooperation and mutual Understanding held before our very eyes when we can think and apply in life hearty unity in the name of the most Significant and most Beautiful! Already the fact is remarkable that we can unitedly repeat the prayer of the Beautiful! Verily, our times are difficult because of all the commotions of the spirit, all non-understanding, and all the attacks of darkness against Light. But perhaps this terrible tension is but the impulse in order to direct humanity through all storms and over all abysses to peaceful construction and mutual respect.

Just think what an unforgettable, epoch-making day is before us when over all the centers of Spirit, Beauty, and Knowledge will be unfurled the one Banner. This banner will call everyone to revere the treasures of the human spirit, to respect culture, and to have a new valuation of labor as the only measure of true values. From childhood, people will witness that there exists not only a flag of the Red Cross, so nobly established for the protection of the health of the human body, but that there also exists a sign of peace and culture for the health of the Spirit.

Above all the treasures of the creations of human genius will wave the Banner, which itself says: "Here are guarded the treasures of all mankind, here, above all petty divisions, above illusory borders of enmity and hatred, as the Fiery Stronghold of Love, Labor, and the all-moving Creation."

People weary of incessant toiling will look up with love to the Sign of Spiritual Communion; the heart of everyone will throb in joy seeing the manifested Sign of Labor, Knowledge, and Beauty. Let everyone in his field, within his possibilities, apply his strength and experience to affirm urgently the Sign of peaceful cooperation. No obstacles, convulsions of hatred, nor falsehood can prevent humanity from striving toward the reverence of true values. The measure of destruction and vandalism is overflowing. Nobody will dare say that this is an exaggeration. Murder, slander, and destruction take place daily. The shame for the black foam of hatred fills the earth. The heart of humanity, of course, realizes that one cannot proceed further by this path. The whispering of hypocrites that the situation is not bad is not convincing for those who see with their own eyes all the horrors around them—not only in times of wars but also in all other times—which through some misunderstanding are called times of peace. The human heart wants real peace. It strives to labor—creatively and actively. It wants to love and expand in the realization of Sublime Beauty. In the highest perception of Beauty and Knowledge, all conventional divisions disappear. The heart speaks its own language; it wants to rejoice at that which is common for all, uplifts all, and leads to the radiant Future.

Is not the Sign of which we all think—the Banner of the radiant Future! We must affirm those great milestones for which we will not be ashamed before any judgment of the future humanity. When we affirm, with the whole power of our spirit, the Banner of protection of the treasures of humanity, we know that the future unseen friends will thank us for it. They will thank us that, during the most difficult hours, we have nevertheless carried high the Banner of Unity, Beauty, and Knowledge and desired to safeguard the treasure troves, not for ourselves, but for those who will come later to this ploughed field of labor.

To transform the dusky life of every day into a continuous Festival of Love and Great Service is an undeferrable and immutable aim. People are responsible for the state of the planet. They cannot justify themselves that in ignorance, delusion, and hatred they have debased the beautiful creations. For such a crime there is no vindication. And if some homunculus would try to seduce you, stating that thoughts about beauty, knowledge, and peace are of no importance, then quickly turn away from this ignoramus and hasten to the Banner of Peace where you will find friends and coworkers. When speaking of coworkers of various cooperative actions, we speak of the actual value of labor. We say that when working in the name of great Culture we want to assemble around an unconquerable Banner, where Love, Trust, and Creativeness find their birth.

Is it not a grand realization to witness creative laborers under the Banner of Peace!

Is it not glorious to see the march of the youth, inspired and enthusiastic, knowing that it goes under the Banner of Peace in the name of the Highest, the most Beautiful!

Himalayas, 1933.

DARKNESS VERSUS SYNTHESIS

[*The Scholar.* Palghat, Vol. IX, No. 4,
January, 1934, pp. 239–242]

HEARTY thanks for all your kind messages[*] in reply to my calls for synthesis. It is joyful and timely that you support in your various articles this undeferrably needed conception.

It would seem that the entire history of humanity directs us once and forever to understand the principles of cooperation, containment, and the harmonization of the centers.[**] But reality shows that things are entirely different. I will not reiterate about the obvious dark forces, to whom every mention about synthesis is adverse and irritating. This is quite natural for chaos, with all its disorderly whirls, that is opposed to harmony, progress, and constructiveness. Thus, we will not be surprised that darkness always is, and will be, against every constructiveness and synthesis. But it is especially deplorable when one witnesses that even certain seemingly cultural minds are disturbed and revolt against every reference to synthesis. Such a slight is so unexpectedly rude and vulgar that one does not even want to believe that under the masks of respectability and sweet voices could hide such fossilized and dusty, outlived ideas. Darkness hopes to break up the light, but encounters are defeated in such absurd attempts.

---

[*]   A message to Swami Jagadiswarananda, our esteemed and regular contributor, concerning his review of Professor Roerich's latest book.

[**]   Nerve centers

All voluntary and involuntary allies of darkness are also certainly defeated in due course. But time is needed to find out every absurdity. It is infinitely sad to witness how valuable, irreplaceable time is wasted on mutual negations and divisions in order not to admit the possibility of healthy, blissful synthesis.

If we will tell ourselves that this deplorable state is the consequence of darkness, it will be a poor consolation. Or if we say that it issues from narrow thinking or envy or malice, then this will be a still poorer consolation because such abhorrent properties are also created by the same darkness. The spreading of darkness is terrible, and it ravages like a pernicious epidemic. Humanity has discovered many salutary remedies against plague, cholera, and similar pestilences, but the microbes of dark negation still have not been found.

Turning to the history of humanity, we see a multitude of examples of the most absurd negations, with the sole purpose to besmirch constructive synthesis. Many stupidities were expressed to the effect that Leonardo da Vinci harmed his great art by being at the same time a remarkable engineer, biologist, and philosopher. And more than once it was hinted, in the most ignorant way, that the art of Rubens suffered from his diplomatic career and statesmanship. However, a mighty creativeness and a wide mind demand multifarious expressions in varied materials and domains. The ordainments of Eastern wisdom tell us that even Bodhisattvas should master at least one art and one craft. The wisdom of ancient rabbis underlines that if the youth, besides its main activity, will not be skilled in some craft, then it will be like preparing them for the banditry of the crossroads.

The whole of antiquity, all epochs of renaissance relate the most striking compatibilities. Let us not forget Cardinal Richelieu, who when searching for an active secretary chose a man who was busy in many fields. And when it was hinted to the cardinal that this man was already too busy for a new appointment, the experienced statesman replied, "If he is so busy, he will know how to also find time for my work." The much-experienced cardinal valued all advantages derived from the realization of synthesis.

We further know that Julius Caesar sometimes dictated six letters simultaneously. Long is the list of such similar examples of containment and compatibilities, which but prove the inexhaustible possibilities of a man.

We heard that Einstein, besides being a brilliant mathematician, is also a wonderful violinist. Has music belittled his astounding mathematical foresight? Certainly not. The harmony of sound gave him new daring thoughts of his definition of the Universe. The remarkable pianist Hoffmann, at the same time, is also an excellent mathematician and engineer. Who will dare to say that one or the other is incompatible and an impeding principle? Spinoza was a skillful master of telescopical lenses and, besides, was known as a fine portraitist. Has his deep philosophy suffered from this, or have his lenses become worse because of his philosophy?

One may enumerate numerous similar examples, in which a thinker also expressed himself in different fields of creativeness and craftsmanship.

It would seem that these facts are sufficiently obvious and dear and that one needn't dwell on them. But humanity, up to now, strives by all means to affirm the unnecessary divisions and perilous specialization.

The horrors of unemployment, the horrors of the inability to properly assign one's time and capacities, are due to such absurd divisions. At the time of the Italian Renaissance, Leonardo and many other masters, endowed with various talents, were recognized; but now, in spite of every kind of human progress, this would call forth many negations and condemnations. I was witness to a discussion that took place as to whether the composer Rachmaninov should also appear as a conductor of a symphony orchestra. According to the opinion of a certain manager, a good composer could not also be a good conductor and *vice versa*. The ideas of the manager were that one should not burden the public with such compatibility. As if the broad masses could in no way understand that a man can act in two fields if they are close to each other in their essence! No doubt the same manager would have condemned Hoffmann for his love for mathematics, or Alexandre Nikolayevich Benois for permitting himself to be at the same time an artist and a writer. No doubt a reference to the famous Italian Vasari, who was both an artist and a historian, would have been of small avail to persuade present-day ignoramuses. Someone even stated the stupidity that an artist cannot be a philosopher—in other words, a clever person—as if creativeness was connected only with idiots; and when it was recently printed in the papers that the Lord Mayor of Bridgeport, who is a skilled roof layer, continued his handicraft even during his municipal activities, then the readers only smiled. From the point of view of the disseminator and the belittler, this was proof of the uselessness of the Lord Mayor in both fields. And what is there bad in the fact that the famous Russian composer Borodin, of *Prince Igor* fame, was a professor of the Military Medical Academy?

You would be horrified if I would whisper to you several names of persons who are very remarkable in their own line, but who judge extremely narrowly about the ability of synthesis for others. The above-mentioned example of the cause of unemployment, as a consequence of narrow specialization, should make critics and deniers think whether it is right to condemn and limit human abilities and possibilities. Man, as a true powerful microcosmos, has in himself infinite expressions and many beautiful qualities. Would inadaptability and limitations correspond to the great aims of the macrocosmos? No doubt if people strive toward progress, then the latter should, first of all, express itself both in cooperation and in synthesis.

Divisions and conventional limitations have reached incredible absurdity. One must have a very poor mind when one directs humanity toward such deadly divisions and prohibitions. Precisely from them is generated a shameful, mutual human hatred, of which we are witness. The study of the nervous system, with its fiery energies, shows what a many-sided instrument the human organism is.

In the name of the highest knowledge, in the name of the betterment of life, in the name of cooperation, we have to acknowledge the hidden properties and possibilities in every human being. And having admitted the existence of these happy qualities, people must find in themselves the moral strength to express themselves, despite the whisperings of darkness, for the good of all, not being held back by prohibition where existence itself commands the possibilities of flourishing containment and synthesis. Especially, let the youth, students from the first days of their studies, hear of synthesis as the true mover of progress.

I rejoice to hear that you in various writings stress synthesis as the foundation of culture. Thus it is! If synthesis is preordained to be vitally realized, then let the best creative elements, without dark negations, unite on the benevolent understanding of synthesis.

Thus, let us keep cordially together. Let us, at last, expel malicious dark denials, and let us find in various fields of life—a radiant unifying concept!

THE WORLD'S DEMARCATION LINE

[*The Buddhist.* Colombo, Vol. V, No. 1-2,
May–June, 1934, pp. 4-6]

MANY testing stones have been given to humanity by the means of which one may discern Light from darkness. Similar to litmus paper, the human face becomes morbid or radiant when tests are mentioned.

When the noble symbol of the Red Cross was proposed, many faces of opposers became morbid. And not only did those who dwell on human hatred turn sullen, but they flashed malice whenever signs of mercy and help were mentioned in their presence. But the defenders of Light were firm, and malice received yet another defeat.

Similarly do some hypocrites make horrible faces when one speaks to them of the protection of treasures of religion, art, and science. Before benevolent symbols, all those shrivel who live on decay and destruction. Look at the names of those who refuse even to discuss salutary measures. They will put up all sorts of obstacles against constructive good and cooperation. Verily, the world has split along the demarcation line, with cooperation and constructiveness on one side and hatred, destruction, and negation on the other.

Also try to mention living ethics, honor, and dignity, and you will witness the same mysterious but striking division. It will be international; neither races, nor nations, nor religions, nor languages may be regarded as indicative signs. In short, one meets Light or darkness.

Try to discuss heroism, leadership, and Guruship, and you will meet the same international demarcation line. Neither age, nor education, nor family surroundings, but entirely different stimuli denote the two opposing camps. Touch on the questions of hygiene of the spirit and body, point out the significance of healthy food, vegetarianism, and the necessity of the purity of life, and out from space will appear before you the same mysterious, almost indescribable, and yet obvious, divisions.

It is very striking that the inhabitants of both camps, despite their difference in clothing and speech, will easily and most friendly meet each other on their own ground. Those who revolted against the Red Cross will smile in welcome of the deniers of the protection of cultural treasures. The deniers of Guruship and heroism will in utmost friendship understand the scoffers of living ethics. And, of course, they will all agree on a bloody beefsteak and a glass of liquor.

Of course, it is also easier for the cooperators of constructiveness to be together. No oceans can divide them in their striving toward the betterment of life. Ethics will be for them the most leading subject, and their feasts will not require any bloodshed. But when the questions of the health of body and spirit will be touched upon, in this respect, also, understanding will not be marred. Everyone will understand that one cannot speak of the health of the body without the convalescence of the spiritual principles. And for this purpose, all will agree that the protection of cultural treasures will be the first measure.

The friends of Goodwill all admit that Good is not an abstract concept. They will also admit that the present situation of the world demands the unification of the epidemic of all such obsessions—people must seek the communion through the heart.

"Depriving of the blessing" is an act of the most ancient patriarch. It is far removed from later curses. A curse is already a product of ignorance, but the ancient act foresaw the severing of the link with Hierarchy. The link with Hierarchy is a true blessing with all its effects. Ignorant ones will say: "How many times have we blasphemed against the Highest, and yet we exist; no fire has consumed us, and nothing threatens us." Then, we will lead them to the marketplace where the blind beggars are groping in the dust: "Behold yourselves!" We will lead them into dungeons, into mines, into conflagrations; we will lead them to executions, and we will say: "Do you not recognize yourselves? As soon as the thread with the Highest was broken, you were precipitated into an abyss." One need not threaten; life is filled with such terrible examples of horrors. Remember that the intensity of the fire is invisible, but nothing can escape consequences. Thus, one can see how even the ancients understood the justice of the law and already knew that the offense against the Highest Principle is so tremendous and terrible that the consequences cannot be immediate.

The wisdom of the world repeatedly warns, "Leprosy begins from a most insignificant spot." But in the camp of darkness, one continues to bear threatening shouts: "To hell with culture," "cash first," and "to hell with idealism." Such shameful cries are uttered when people try to protect the real treasures of mankind. Such shouts sound even incredible after all the cultural accumulations of centuries. But darkness was seldom so active as at present. One could seldom see in the past such real international darkness, as in our days, when ignorant masses are being conducted along all rituals of hell.

But if the forces of darkness understand their unity and their Hierarchy, then is it not high time that the servitors of Light also unite upon their watchtowers for the incessant vigil? The demarcation line of Light and darkness stands out clearly, especially in the days of spiritual battle when darkness roars in wrath, but the light-bearers are exalted in spirit and undaunted courage.

There is no such abyss that cannot be filled with creative good and turned into a beautiful garden. But for such gardening, one must understand real cooperation. I send my greetings to these gardeners of Light.

Himalayas, 1934.

ISWARA

[*The Vedanta Kesari.* Madras, Vol. XXI, No. 8,
December, 1934, pp. 295-299]

A Dedication

Oh, Thou unlimited by space,
Existing Thou in matter churning,
Primordial to flow of time,
Impersonal—Divinity Triune!
Spirit, Thou One, and Omnipresent,
Without abode, nor having cause,
Whom no one has conceived as yet!
All with His presence filling,
Who all contains, creates, preserves,
And whom we glorify as God!

THUS, in literary translation, sounds the beginning verse of the immortal poem of the first Russian poet, Derjavin, written by him in 1784.

"And in Heaven I see—God!" exclaimed another great Russian poet.

The Credo begins: "I believe in One God, the Father Almighty, Creator of Heaven and Earth, and everything visible and invisible." Toward the Highest of the Highest, to the Breath of all Breathing, to the Atman of all Existence, all nations in all languages bring their sacred and immutable striving. Everyone within the limits of his heart, within the boundaries of his understanding of the Beautiful, dedicates the best names to Elohim. May these sacred names be manifold; but assembled into One, they sound in an inspiringly touching symphony of all that is the best—of all that is the Highest—which could express the human mind and inscribe the embodied hand with all the most sacred hieroglyphs.

The sacred immutability of God the Almighty is born in the brain of every child when it first sees the splendor of the stars and thus turns toward the Infinite Worlds. This enlightened thought brings to the same eternal radiant conception: "My father has many Mansions." And another formula as limitless in its greatness is affirmed:

"But the hour cometh, and now is when the true worshipper shall worship the Father in spirit and in truth; for the Father seeketh such to worship him." (John 4: 23–24).

A book under the title *Has Science Discovered God? A Symposium of Modern Scientific Opinion*, compiled by E. H. Cotton, has just appeared. In this book are collected the opinions of the foremost scientists about God. Amongst the renowned names we see Millikan, Einstein, Oliver Lodge, Thomson, Byrd, Curtiss, Eddington, Jeans, and Mather. Each one of them, in his own way, glorifies this Highest all-unifying Conception, without which the very idea of the greatness of Infinity would be impossible.

The time has already passed when in the name of some false scientific materialism the great Realities were refuted. Atheism, in the history of humanity, appeared as a paroxysm of despair when man—due to his own faults—found himself in complete darkness and lost all understanding of the surroundings, the great forms, and the meaning of fundamental principles. The last generation sometimes still admitted the self-conceited, desecrated formula that except for themselves nothing exists. All far-off worlds were for them only lamps for their own delight, and even the sun was, of course, only a source of their personal comfort.

Notorious for his atheism, Bazaroff stupidly

exclaimed that after his death only burdock will grow out of him! Yet such silly exclamations were not peculiar expressions of self-modesty. On the contrary, they wanted, thereby, to affirm their bodily, materialistic finality, being full of conceit in their relative and materialistic knowledge. Such a negative type is described by Turgenev in his famous novel *Fathers and Sons.* Turgenev understood well the fallacy of such ideas. Another Russian writer, Dostoevsky, approaches the same subject by giving a type of would-be peasant atheism. This writer describes an atheist soldier who, wishing to produce the utmost desecrated action in order to convince himself of the non-existence of God, placed a most sacred Church object on a pillar and shot at it. At the moment of this sacrilege, he saw the vision of Christ Himself appearing at the very place. In this example, would-be atheism is described as a peculiar evocation of God, a prayer for a miracle of a holy sign that had always existed in the depths of the heart. Thus, the human heart understands, in its innermost depth, that every form of destruction is negative.

We have before us a significant, recently issued book of the miracles that occurred during the last years. In this book are compiled facts certified by many witnesses and also mentioned in the press. These subtle manifestations are detailed at length, with particulars about the quality of radiance occurring during these phenomena and with all effects and impressions upon the many witnesses. Elsewhere, there are similar records about the miraculous healings at Lourdes. And, again, we have information that in 1925 in the town of Kostroma on the Volga river, an aged monk passed away in whose paper records we found about a path to the sanctuaries of the Holies of Himavat. The Siberian Old Believers, an orthodox sect retaining ancient Christian belief, still go on pilgrimage to the sacred Belovodye,

"White Waters," and are striving to the highest communion with God. On the same path one meets the *don-dam don-pa*, the so-called highest form of Understanding of Buddhist-Tibetan consciousness.

As soon as one leaves the path of senseless negation and strives on the path of Good, on the path of radiant creative thought, one is overwhelmed by the innumerable facts and signs from all peoples of the whole world—the value of which will be, at once, perceived by the pure heart. All nations seeking God and manifesting God know in their hearts, also, of a glorious future. Messiah, Maitreya, Kalki-Avatar, Muntazar, Mitolo, and Saoshyant—everyone, in his own way and according to the best of his understanding, expects this radiant future, sending his heartfelt prayer to the One God Almighty. In Isphagan, the White Steed for the Great Advent is already saddled. A rabbi in Hamadan will say, "You are also Israel if you search for the Light!" Brahmins are coming in order to celebrate together with you amid spring flowers the great Sri Krishna. Every one of them, in his own way striving toward the good and the Blessed Future, knows God.

In a remarkable book, *On Eastern Crossroads* by J. St. Hilaire, is quoted an inspiring saying about the veneration of the Guru:

"I recall a small Hindu who found his Teacher. We asked him, 'Is it possible that the sun would glow to you if you would see it without the Teacher?'

"The boy smiled: 'The sun would remain as the sun; but in the presence of the Teacher, twelve suns would shine to me!'

"The sun of the wisdom of India shall shine because upon the shores of a river there sits a boy who knows the Teacher."

In this hearty veneration of the Hierarchy of Light is manifested an unwavering belief in God; even more so is manifested not only the belief but even a realization of God, which leads not only to God-seeking but to the manifestation of God. The knowledge of the omnipresence of God, existing in every grain of sand, not only does not belittle the Greatness but, on the contrary, gives reality to all subtle conditions, to all far-off worlds, to everything perceived by the human eyes, and, moreover, to everything that the human heart knows in its innermost depth. The Heart—the Sun of suns, this altar of the Almighty! Verily, not for long have science and great religions been parted. All new discoveries of energies, rays, waves, rhythm, glories unseen to the eye, and riches of the actual Might of God, again attract every honest study that, unfailingly, leads one along the infinite Hierarchy of Light; and ascends toward the highest, beautiful regions where neither petty earthly divisions nor malice and hatred exist but where the Great Agni-Fire of creative Thought eternally shines. In the radiance of the great Thought of the Almighty, the human thought is also enlightened by the flame of the awakening Heart.

Up to now, Western science has attributed to the heart only physiological functions, ignoring its higher meaning as the transmuter of the subtlest energies, which incessantly pass through it and nourish and refine the consciousness. The Hindus know from old traditions that the great Manas has its abode in the heart; and, not without reason, Hindus, when speaking of thought, place their hand on the heart. Thus, the apparatus of the brain, sometimes forcibly divided from the activity of the heart, again becomes a true coworker of reality. And in this turning to cooperation is again expressed the great conception of the omnipresence of the Spirit, of God. The conception of cooperation, predestined to humanity for the glorious future, is indeed close to the true realization of God. Those strong in spirit were not frightened at the responsibility of the formula of the Imitation of God. *The Imitation of Christ* by Thomas A. Kempis contains in no way self-conceit but is a call toward highest cooperation!

The East, with its ancient traditions, watched with amazement the attempts of science to separate itself from the Highest. For it was in the East that the heart was acknowledged as the first conductor to the Altar of God. The hermits of Mt. Sinai, all prophets, and all Rishis imbued by their striving toward God knew the highest possibilities of our spiritual guide—the human heart.

Swami Vivekananda justly says that some of the modern thinkers, because of the diversity of understanding of conceptions, raised the question of whether it is not necessary to replace the word *God* with some other definition. But the wise Swami, of course, arrives at the conclusion that in this term are accumulated so many of the highest human strivings that its deep reality should not be touched. Indeed, every blasphemous substitute would be similar to primitive searching when the human mind, still bound by many crude circumstances, tried to bring the conception of the Infinite Greatness to its own earthly conditional understanding and definitions.

The conception of God—this infinite number of highest qualities—is, of course, inexpressible through our earthly limited vocabulary. But the Heart in its own unlimited language knows this highest wisdom of Infinity—the rays of which play on the Lotus of Consciousness. I remember how one of my late dear friends, the renowned poet Alexander Block, ceased to visit the Religious Philosophical Society. On being questioned about the reason for his absence, he answered: "Because they speak there of the Unspeakable!" This great Unspeakable, Indescribable, was for him a reality. And, indeed, with his fine sensing of a poet, he felt the rudeness of the verbal disputes of so High, Fine, and Infinite a conception that sounds only in the heart. Every word about God already inflicts some blasphemous limitation to this untold Greatness.

Now is a special time to remember God, to remember the Commandments of old Ordainments, to remember the Indescribable, Unspeakable, Undefinable, and Infinite and, at the same time, to remember what is so near to us—what saturates every human heart when it thinks of the Common Good. How beautifully is expressed the Divine Omnipresence in the best Commandments!

The world is shattered by all kinds of crises. In this misery, in this poverty, once more the Great Conception is raised that, if only partly realized, would transmute human life into a beautiful garden. Breaking away from God, breaking away from the free, unbound radiant knowledge, and breaking away from the predestined joy of perfection would turn the significant life of this world into an Island of Tears. Yet our lot is not misery; unhappiness is not predestined. The highest joy, the creative tremor of thought, and the fragrance of the Altar of the Heart are ordained. Not an Island of Tears but a beautiful Garden—a Garden of transformed Labor and Knowledge is the domain of all people who turn toward God.

Derjavin concludes his poem "God" with the following lines:

> Creator, I am thy creation!
> I am the being of Thy Wisdom!
> Thou Giver of the Blissful Source of Life,
> Thou Spirit of my soul, and King!

To Thy Wisdom it was needed
That my immortal Be-ness pass
Through the abysses of death;
That my soul be clad in mortality
And that through death I should rejoin
Thy Immortality, Oh Bather.
Oh Inexplainable! Beyond Conception!

I know that useless are
Imaginations of my soul
To draw Thy shadow;
But if glorification be,
Then helpless mortals
Cannot better express esteem,
Than raising up themselves to Thee,
To disappear in forms immortal
And render grateful tears.

PEACE UNTO THE WHOLE WORLD

[*Prabuddha Bharata.* Calcutta, April, 1935, pp. 183–184]

WOULD it not appear that to pray "for peace of the whole world" is the greatest utopia? This seems evident. But the heart and the real being continues to reiterate these sacred words as a possible reality. If one listens to the voice of superficial obviousness, then even all the Commandments will seem a utopia, impossible to carry out in life. Where is "Thou shalt not kill"? Where is "Thou shalt not steal"? Where is "Thou shalt not commit adultery"? Where is the fulfillment and carrying out of all the simple and clear commandments of Life? Perhaps some wiseacres will say, "Why reiterate these commands if, anyhow, they are not carried out!"

Every one of us has often heard various complaints and warnings against utopia. From childhood and youth, one has heard the *experienced advice* not to be carried away by *empty idealism* but to keep closer to *practical life.* Some young hearts did not agree with this *practical life,* to which the wiseacres tried to persuade them. Some youths heard the voice of their hearts whispering that the path to idealism, against which the elder ones were warning, is the most vital and preordained. On this ground of idealism and *conventional wisdom,* many family tragedies have taken place. Who knows what was the cause of many suicides—of these most foolish solutions to life's problems. For the wiseacres did not warn the youth in the time of the terrible delusion, which even led to suicide. And when these gradually doomed young men asked the elders whether during the alleged *practical life*, the Commandments will be carried out, the elder ones, sometimes with a cynical gesture, sacrilegiously murmured, "Everything will be forgiven." And between this "everything will be forgiven" and the Commandments of Life, there arose some insoluble contradiction. The wiseacres were ready to promise everything if only to prevent the youth from idealism. And when the youth submerged into conventional, mechanical life, then even the scribes and Pharisees threw up their hands. But the question arises: Who took the youth to boxing matches, races, and obscene films? And did not the *wise councilors* themselves constantly repeat, with a sign, "Without cheating, one cannot sell," and thus did they not themselves zealously create these decaying conditions of life? It was once said, "Today a small compromise, tomorrow another small compromise, and the following day—a great scoundrel."

Precisely in this way, in the smallest compromises against radiant idealism, has the imagination and consciousness been polluted. The dark consciousness began to whisper of the inapplicability of the Commandments to life. And precisely this viper of doubt began to assure, in the darkness of the night, that the peace of the whole world is a mere utopia.

But this prayer was already, ages ago, laid down, not as an abstractness but as an imperative call for a possible reality! The Great Minds knew that the peace of the whole world is not only possible but also that peace is that great salutary magnet, to which sooner or later the ships of all travelers will be attracted. In different languages, at various ends of the world, this sacred prayer is and will be reiterated. Inscrutable are the ways, and it is not for man to prejudge how, where, and when idealism will become a reality. Verily, the ways cannot be foretold. But the final goal remains one! And to this goal will lead all manifestations of that idealism that is so often persecuted by wiseacres. There will also come the day when so-called idealism will be understood not only as something most practical but even as the sole path for the solution of all other problems of life. The same idealism will also create a striving to honest, unlimited knowledge as one of the most salutary harbors. Idealism will disperse superstition and prejudices that so fatally deaden the vital strivings of mankind. If someone would collect an encyclopedia of superstitions and prejudices, this would disclose the strange truth that many of the vipers, up to now, live even amid that humanity that considers itself enlightened.

But above all confusions, the angels sing of peace and goodwill. No guns, no explosives can silence these choirs of heaven. And despite all the earthly pseudo-wisdom, idealism as the Teaching of Goodwill still remains the quickest reaching and the most easily reached and most renewing principle in life. It has been said, "O generation of vipers, how can ye, being evil, speak of good things?" Precisely evil-heartedness will whisper that every act of goodwill is impractical and untimely. But let us know firmly that even peace unto the whole world is not an abstraction but depends only on the desire and goodwill of humanity. Thus, every admonition to safeguard the Highest and the best is exactly most timely and alleviates the shortest path.

May the beneficial symbols, may the Banner of Goodwill be unfurled over everything, by which the human spirit exists.

"Glory to God in the highest, peace on earth, and goodwill toward men!"

INEXHAUSTIBILITY

[*The Maha-Bodhi.* Calcutta, Vol. XLIII, No. 5,
May, 1935, pp. 232–235]

D OES inexhaustibility exist?
On the physical plane, everything can be exhausted, but on the spiritual plane—at the base of everything—lies inexhaustibility. And according to this measure, the two planes are primarily divided. When we are told that something has become exhausted, we know that this pertains to purely physical conditions.

A creator imagines that his creativeness is at an end, and this is, of course, untrue. Simply, there are, or there have arisen, some reasons that impeded creativeness. Perhaps something has taken place that harmed the free flow of creativeness. But, in itself, creativeness, when once called forth into action, is inexhaustible. Likewise, psychic energy, as such, is ever flowing and cannot be impeded.

In the confused life of today, this simple fact must constantly be remembered. People insist that they have become tired, and they suggest to themselves that their creative ability is at an end. Repeating in various terms about difficulties, they actually wrap themselves into a veritable cobweb. Space is really filled with a multitude of harmful crosscurrents. They can influence the physical side of manifestation. But to people who are accustomed to building everything within physical bounds, it always seems that these outer intrusions kill the very essence of their psychic energy. Yet even this very expression will often seem as something indefinite because people, up until now, seldom ponder over this fundamental blessed energy, which is inexhaustible and ever-present when realized.

In general, the question concerning tangibility is very unclear to human consciousness. One repeatedly hears how a person may give, at times, quite definite data, but the listeners with their uneducated attention are unable to grasp them and then assure that they were given something abstract that cannot be applied. I have often witnessed how people gave precise information founded on facts, and yet they were told: "Can't we have something more to the point, more practical, and definite?" Such questions only show that the interlocutor had no intention to accept everything that had been said to him, but he wanted to hear only that which he, for some reason, expected. And under this self-suggestion, he often was unable to appreciate all the precise facts that were told to him. How often do people desire to hear not that which is, but that which they want to hear? "Verily, he is deaf who does not want to hear!"

The nondesire to listen and to see gives rise not only to great injustice but often it is as if a spiritual suicide. A person will hypnotize himself to such an extent that he is unable to do something; and to such an extent, he will suppress his basic energy so that he really falls under the sway of all outer physical, as well as psychic, intrusions.

Everyone has heard how often persons with so-called nervous diseases cannot cross a street nor approach a window, or, again, they become subject to the horror of suspicion. If one investigates how these fatal symptoms began, one can always find an insignificant, often hardly perceptible, suppression of psychic energy. At times it will be caused indirectly and may begin from something quite unexpected.

Precisely such accidents could have been easily avoided if attentiveness to everything that takes place around us would have been developed. This attentiveness would help us to notice that the basic energy is inexhaustible. This simple and clear realization would save many from the abyss of despair and disillusion. Thus, a person who suffers from insomnia will often find the cause of it in the most real, external conditions. Likewise, man will understand why it has been repeated from antiquity that "it is difficult to make oneself think; it is still more difficult to abstain from thinking."

When man extinguishes his enthusiasm, he does so because of some purely external conditions. If with all attentiveness he would realize how accidental and ephemeral are these circumstances, he would chase them away like an annoying fly. But children are not taught attentiveness, neither at school nor in the family; and yet, later on, one is surprised why one cannot see a forest on account of the bushes. But, then, does one often speak in the family circle about the fire of the heart, about inspiration, and enthusiasm? Too often the family gathering is confined only to mutual condemnation and malicious criticisms. Nevertheless, from ancient times, from everywhere, the calls and commands reach us to preserve, in purity, the wells of inspiration and creativeness—as in thought, so in action.

"Raj-Agni, thus, was called that Fire, which you call enthusiasm. Truly, this is a beautiful and powerful Fire that purifies all the surrounding space. The constructive thought is nurtured upon this Fire. The thought of magnanimity grows in the silvery light of the Fire Raj-Agni. Help to the near ones flows from the same source. There are no limitations, no bounds to the wings radiant with Raj-Agni. Do not think that this Fire will be kindled in an evil heart. One must develop in oneself the ability to call forth the source of such transport.

At first, you must develop in yourself the assurance that you offer your heart to the Great Service. Then one ought to think that the glory of the works is not yours but belongs to the Hierarchy of Light. Then one may become uplifted by the infiniteness of Hierarchy and affirm oneself in the heroic achievement needed for all worlds. Thus, not for oneself but in the Great Service, Raj-Agni is kindled. Understand that the Fiery World cannot exist without this Fire."

JUSTICE

[*The Scholar.* Palghat, Vol. X, No. 11, August, 1935, pp. 549–551]

PEOPLE often speak of obvious injustices, and, at the same time, they lose sight of the signs of justice. Of course, injustice is quite obvious and tangible, and justice often manifests itself so very indirectly that narrow thinking can, with difficulty, collate the different, often disconnected, manifestations. Truly, the paths of justice are often much more unexpected than the actions of injustice. Such expectancy is, of course, only a seeming one. Truth follows the logical course, but the scope of its actions transcends the human horizon.

Man commits some obvious vile injustice. Casual observers see that the perverter of truth not only continues to exist but even seems to be distinguished as if encouraged. For the human measures, it is difficult to realize that these phantom distinctions are but the road to the gallows. The criminal himself continues to rejoice, thinking in his debasity that his criminal machinations have fully succeeded and that the hand of Nemesis cannot reach him. But it is also said: "Vengeance is mine; I will repay."

Even some considerable time may pass, and around the criminal—whether it be a person, a group, or a country—there will accumulate some strange, quite unforeseen, and incalculable circumstances. The very distinctions and seeming successes begin to change into unexpected unpleasantnesses. Of course, criminal thinking will not pay attention to these small forewarning flashes. In the drunkenness of an orgy of boasting, the evil ones cannot collate and correctly value the seemingly unconnected distant lightning.

Some very instructive, unusual psychological moments take place, which can lead the thinker to unusual deductions. But, in order to come to such conclusions, one must have not only an ability to concentrate, but one must have first of all clean thinking. And it is precisely this quality that is absent in the criminal. One can see that even when some calamity begins to fall upon them, they still remain far from realizing the true causes.

The inexperienced people will ask, why does justice often seem to tarry? This question only proves that the inquirer could not go beyond the bounds of the usual. It is only here, under our conditions, that the dates appear to us as short or protracted. But there also exist other higher and far more refined scales. And when the human mind succeeds in grasping these fine processes of correspondence, combinations, and effects, then a special tremor will arise. The tremor of realization of the signs of Justice. The ancient wisdom says: "It is better to be offended than to be the offender."

In this is expressed a knowledge of the laws of effects. And the date of the process itself cannot be comprehended by earthly measures.

Only when looking back, a jurist-philosopher can weigh and collate in exaltation.

Nil admirare (admire nothing). The Romans expressed thus not only their satiated, cold attitude but also the knowledge of correspondence. One cannot be surprised at justice. One may admire these high laws, which in their harmony attract or repel something, yet the beautiful fire of justice will always reign. The criminal burns himself with this fire. Precisely he is singed; that is to say, he singes himself. He himself approaches the fire. He cannot avoid the path of justice.

People believe that a murderer is attracted to the place of the murder. In this is contained a deep wisdom of the people. The criminal is attracted not only to the physical place, but he himself becomes involved in the orbit of issuelessness. In his dullness, the criminal will imagine for some time that he avoids situations that are dangerous for him. It will seem to him that he not only succeeded in escaping his nemesis but even received an unquestionable benefit from the committed evil deed.

"When God wants to punish someone, He deprives him of his reason." Precisely the clouding of the brain follows the evil deeds. It is vain to think that actions of hatred and malice remain without retribution. The evildoers call upon themselves terrible consequences. And every evil, as a spot of rust, eats into the fate of the creator. It penetrates all the deeper, for so-called repentance comes very seldom. On the contrary, a hardened bluntness will try to justify the crime.

It is said that in a certain ancient country, all sage-philosophers were called together in order to observe the ways of justice. It may be only a legend to emphasize the meaning of these paths and the actuality of justice, but perhaps this took place in reality. Among the ancient cultures, we often meet examples of unusually high thought.

Amid the subjects of living ethics, the word about the paths of justice must be especially convincing. It will teach the young generation from their school years to realize the whole impracticability of evil deeds.

SEEDS OF BLISS

[*The Twentieth Century.* Allahabad, June, 1935, pp. 503–505]

HERE are groups of youths who gathered in the name of beautiful, constructive beginnings—in the highest names and understandings—the most valuable centers of the working youth, who struggle with difficulty against their own straitened existence. And no matter how these seekers of the best spiritual strongholds search, they cannot find even a minimum sum in order to strengthen the existence of their unity. Weakened, they will scatter, driven by want. And when will one be able to unite them again—such valuable ones, who so rejoice in the spirit and in the heart?

Here is a cultural society, which is striving toward the tasks of education, culture, and motherhood, toward the strengthening of all those principles that, if unrealized and unconstructed, will cause us again to suffer a spiritual crash as well as a material one.

They are asking so little in order to exist! They give, as it is, everything that belongs to them that can be given. But these most beautiful examples of self-sacrifice are being broken before those icy currents about which the *Transmuting Fire* speaks.

And sometimes even a well-known author, widely praised, cannot write because he has no means of livelihood. Does this not express humanity's mad dissipation of its spiritual forces? And not only do all these manifold requests for the support of beautiful foundations remain unanswered because of want, but the universal order of things continues to tread the same destructive directions of sundering the best cultural projects and aspirations of mankind. And the serious thing is that this pertains not only to one country—or even to a group of countries—no, this unwelcome news unquestionably comes from all parts of the world. Someone will say, "But schools continue to exist, universities continue to exist, and museums also exist." Yes, but let us see what the budgets of these institutions have gradually been reduced to, institutions that are being preserved only for the sake of longevity.

We read daily about the closing of entire scientific departments of museums, about the ceasing of research work, about the ceasing of excavations, about the stopping of construction, about the diminishing of the staffs through which so many needed, irreplaceable young forces are being cut away in order to forever be lost in the ruthless ocean of chaos. *No* and *impossible* prevail. Denials and abolishments rule, even without special discussions that are most necessary. Even in the endowed institutions, we see unprecedented notices about unfulfilled editions, about the delaying of plans, and again about the curtailing of even the most essential.

Of course, we must think about the future—of that no one will have another opinion. Even a manufacturer does not produce for yesterday. And now, amid the same existing ideas about the future, it would seem that people themselves will begin to cut away everything, even that which is fundamentally necessary for every production.

The world has experienced many crashes and shocks. But is there not some sign of the spiritual and material misfortune that has now fallen upon mankind? Such a sign exists. And this sign will be terrible if special attention is not paid to it. This is the sign of universal misfortune. Heretofore, misfortunes were national or

local, but now has come an unprecedented international-
ism of misfortune. There is not one country, there is
not one distant island that does not repeat its tales of
misfortune.

The more in contact you come with the most varied
peoples, the more shocked you are by the universality
of misfortune. The small groups of those who lived on
incomes that veiled the world with an illusory guar-
anty have become absolutely insignificant. Any of those
who do not suffer as yet already speak about misfortune.
And through these misfortunes, carrying affirmations
and actions, comes forth some destructive invocation of
misfortunes, as if some invisible sowers of misfortune
were passing through all the countries and throwing
into space destructive, deadly formulas.

And following them appears a veritable dance of
death: "Cut down, arrest, kill, and deaden." These
deadly words, in many languages and various formulas,
are being carried all over the world. The phantom of
economy has given birth to an army of unemployed and
has brought wages to a standard that does not answer
even the most beggarly needs. Before us are the figures
of various wages, and one must confess that these figures are terrible.

One thing is clear: if mankind continues to hypnotize
itself by invoking misfortune, it will violate that which
is most valuable for its very existence. It will disrupt
Culture; it will disrupt the progress and accumulation
of that which under different conditions is irrevocable
or demands many centuries for curing.

The horror of refusal, the horror of killing living
sprouts can no longer continue. It is absolutely necessary to cast aside personal quarrels and personal rivalry
and to think unitedly about the future generations for
whom the foundation of Culture is the only stronghold of the spirit. Instead of calling forth misfortunes,

sooner or later—and better it should be sooner—it is necessary to turn to the invocation of the foundation of positive construction. Thus, we will begin to solve many so-called insoluble problems. Edison lived long; Michelson also lived long, and none of these creators of thought contemplated suicide. Creative thought is the accumulator of high energies that feeds all saps of life. The high energies of creativeness constitute the great elixir of life eternally sought by men. And this elixir of life proclaims to each one who desires to think, that it is necessary to turn from the destructive invocation of misfortunes to the insistent call of benevolent, cultural constructiveness. And if we will call for the necessity of the development of knowledge and ennoblement, this call will in itself be the first stone in the new construction of the positive stronghold of mankind.

We began with the horror and necessity of refusals; let us end with heartfelt joy about the reality of the possibility of construction, even if it will be only temporarily—even if partially it will be left aside the malice of destruction and decomposition. The creation of the thoughtform is being transmuted into an active one. Therefore, one wants so greatly to tell all workers of Culture, who have recently received so many refusals and curtailments: "Let us hold out, let us not scatter, let us cherish even the remnants of friendliness, and let us cover the refusals by these seeds of Bliss."

To transform the island of tears into a beautiful garden, into a garden of labor and knowledge—is this not the first foundation of all positive Teachings of the World?

DRUNKEN VANDALS

[*The Young Builder*. Karachi, Vol. III, No. 10,
October, 1935, pp. 1–4]

WHAT horrible news! Not to be remembered! The headline alone is unbelievable!

DRUNKEN VANDALS IN THE CITY OF BUDAPEST HAVE DESTROYED AN ANCIENT CHURCH!

"Budapest, January 10: A revolting crime that ended in the burning down of an ancient church and the murder of a priest, took place last night after a peasants' drinking party near Budapest. Completely drunk, several peasants began to bet on the most sensational crime they could do in the vicinity of the city. Someone proposed to burn down the church, and everyone at once rushed to the place and began to set it afire.

"The priest tried to bring them to their senses, but the desperate drunkards threw him aside with such a force that he fell down and broke his skull. Amid hysterical shouts, the beast-like vandals set fire to the church and ran away. All efforts of the local fire brigade to put the fire out failed, and in an hour's time, the monument of great historical interest was reduced to ashes."

Having read of this contemporary horror, how can one say that the time of Herostratus has passed and that human consciousness has outgrown the animal state? It is noteworthy that this insane brutality was directed precisely against a church. Likewise, of all the paintings in the Louvre, a barbarian chooses to mutilate just a painting of such high, spiritual mood—Millet's *Angelus*.

Of course, there may be explanations that every brutality and evil obsession, every criminality, first of all, revolts against all truly spiritual strivings. But such an explanation does not in any way justify the horror of these crimes against the Most High.

When one repeatedly reads such horrible news, no one can succeed in persuading you that the Pact for the Protection of Cultural Treasures of Humanity is not necessary or that it is untimely. Let us also not forget that only a few such vandalisms come to light and that many more remain unreported and sink into the abyss of dark ignorance. Quite recently, we heard that some old mutilated icons were found in Shanghai. Again, some evil one not only repudiated them but even spent his energy on sacrilegious mutilation. If these icons were simply useless to him, this evil biped could have simply tried to sell them or get rid of them, but he did not try to do so. His perversity, his obsession, demanded an active blasphemy. He would rather spend his last means on the acquisition of tools for this barbaric mutilation than to simply give away something of which he is not in need. There is no question here about something not being needed; here we see militant savagery.

Is it not time to remind the people urgently of the foundations of culture? Is it not time to affirm the new impulse of respect for the spiritual treasures of humanity—of respect to that by which people perfect themselves?

If we see such callous destruction and mutilation, then how can one calmly put away decisions in matters that will help to preserve the Sublime and the Beautiful? There are no such self-assured madmen who would dare to say that everything fares well with the monuments of culture. The dark forces—which in many cases despite their small number appear to be very well organized—openly proclaim the destruction of all temples, the uselessness of museums, and the eradication of all Raphaels. When hymns extolling the sweetness of hatred are being composed, should words of Love and Creativeness keep silent? He who advocates hatred cannot belong to Culture!

Rather one must address oneself to the task of constructiveness and watchful protection. From antiquity, we have many examples of tragic delays. While we will still be thinking of the ratification of the Pact for the Protection of Cultural Treasures, the vandals, and even drunken ones, will act with all precipitateness. May the tragic saying about the death of the great poet, Firdausi, not repeat itself again. Just before the death of the poet, Sultan Mahmud became enraptured by a beautiful verse from the *Shah-Namah*, and he learned that the verse had been taken from a book by Firdausi dedicated to him and that Firdausi was in poverty. The Sultan gave orders to send to Firdausi a caravan laden with the richest gifts, but when the Sultan's treasures entered the gates of the city, the dead body of Firdausi was being carried out through another gate. The old legend reminds us of the startling belatedness.

If the ratification of our Pact is going to be delayed and pushed about from one secretariat to another, let us beware that during the interval no regrettable events occur. Peter the Great used to say: "Delay is equal to death!"—and no one who understands the significance of cultural treasures can find an excuse in saying that the matter is not so urgent. The wild vandals, besides being drunk, do not slumber!

SENSITIVENESS

[*Prabuddha Bharata*. Calcutta, Vol. XL, No. 11,
November, 1935, pp. 529–530]

IT is said that water having performed its work in a mill gives the impression of having less force than that of water that flows on to the wheel. As if it is presupposed that, besides the coarse physical conditions, some sort of energy has escaped during the tension. Of course, this is an illusion. Likewise is it said that a book that is new and unread contains greater potentiality than a read book—as if many eyes could extract from the pages some sort of potentiality.

Yet, at the same time, it is justly said of objects that have been prayed over, of objects that have been enwrapped and, thus, strengthened by thought. Consequently, it seems that if something can be imparted to an object through thought, if something is added to the object, then it would appear that likewise, by means of thought and energy, one could deprive an object of something and take it away from the same.

We have heard that someone on opening a book that was returned to him, said, "It is even unpleasant to take it into one's hands; probably some scoundrel read it!" Perhaps this exclamation was caused by suspicion, but perhaps some influence was indeed felt.

Thus, often some unexplainable enmity and sometimes some indescribable goodwill is felt in space itself. Again, some sensitive people will say, "How heavy it is to be in this room!" Or on the contrary, "How easy it is to breathe here!" If even ordinary photographs, at times, bear the most unexpected impressions, if a chemical analysis of space is ready to disclose many things, why should we then be astonished if the finest human apparatus can fully feel the presence of such or other energies?

At times, a stringed instrument seems to resound to influences imperceptible to the human eye. At times, a porcelain vase will break itself from vibrations almost inaudible to the human ear. Sand assumes the most remarkable designs from vibrations almost imperceptible. Likewise, the presence of many influences will not be expressed by words but will be felt by the inner human apparatus.

This will not be superstition nor superficial suspicion. This precisely will be straight knowledge. No amount of verbal explanation will dissuade a man who has clearly felt the contact of these energies. Just as you would be unable to persuade a person that he has not seen something that he has definitely and attentively seen with his own eyes.

It is, at times, considered even a shameful weakness to admit these definite perceptions, and yet they will quietly mention that the food seemed too salty or bitter, whereas their companion has not found it to be so. For one, this quality was not worth noticing, while the other fully sensed it. If only people would just as naturally and fearlessly pay attention and report to their near ones their impressions, how many more new and valuable observations would enrich earthly life and bring a greater eagerness to the transmutation of these sensations into knowledge!

It is impossible to place the means of acquiring knowledge into some predetermined boundaries. Truly, the Messenger comes unexpectedly. Not without reason do all the Teachings point so definitely to these unexpected higher realizations. Yet people always insist that the Messenger should come at the hour appointed by them through a definite door, bringing news expected by them, and probably should speak to them in that tongue and in those expressions that are anticipated by the expecting one.

Every change in this self-appointed program would introduce confusion and perchance would even lead to negation. How could this happen when I did not expect it? Again, this unfortunate and limited "I," which desires to command in a narrow, self-assured way within the boundaries of the visible and audible world. And what if suddenly the most pompous turns out to be a complete nullity before the smallest manifestation of the subtle order? Can one limit that which will not be restricted into any definable bounds?

How many Messengers could not altogether enter because, having approached the doors, they already knew that it was not they who were expected! Repeating to themselves the most God-given and inspiring message, the Messenger already knew that it would not be accepted in this tongue. How much of the already constructed and near-at-hand was arrested by haughty narrow-mindedness? But if you try to define the bounds of this narrow-mindedness in any dimension, you will never find its limits to such an extent that it is thoroughly insignificant.

Thus, amid the most remarkable illuminations and inspirations, intrude—as if gray dust—innumerable fragments of ignorance. Let every particle of dust be imponderable in weight, but a layer of them can darken the most exquisite flower. The common work, the common care, should be that in every household there should be as little of this dust as possible.

WORK

[*East & West.* Hyderabad, Vol. I, No. 4, July, 1936, pp. 104–106]

"HE who does not work has no right to eat."
Very often, the East and West—all over the world—have repeated this wise saying, and yet how often has it been misinterpreted! Everyone tried to explain the meaning of work in his own way. The bootmaker understood that real work was bootmaking; the smith was convinced that true labor was contained in his hammer. The reaper extolled the sickle as the only tool of labor. The scientist naturally understood that work took place in his laboratory, and the warrior insisted that military experience was the only work. Of course, from their point of view, one could not contradict them, but, judging from their ego, they always preferred to think of themselves and not of others.

The work of the neighbor always was regarded through belittling glasses. No one wanted to understand that all kinds of labor are honorable and cooperate with each other. And cooperation was, at any rate, neglected.

Is it not simple? No doubt it is. Is it not known to everybody? Yes, to all—from young to old. Is it applied in life? No, it is not!

There has resulted a self-imposed division of labor into the higher and the lower. And no one wants to ponder where the boundaries and evaluations of work are. Nowadays, people often judge very peculiarly about the quality of work. In view of the development of mechanical output, people rely entirely upon machinery. But even at the base of every machine, there will lie the quality of work according to whether the machine is skillfully used or otherwise.

It has been stated more than once that even machines work differently in the hands of various people. More than that, it is known that some workmen act beneficially upon the machines, whereas others have a destructive influence. From ancient times, people understood the significance of rhythm in labor. We witnessed how for certain public works, local orchestras were engaged to increase the tempo of labor. Even in the remote Himalayan forests, timber carriers carry beams under the rhythmical beating of drums. Many such useful examples can be cited by everybody, and, still, the conscious synchronization of labor is neglected by the multitude.

It is not superfluous to repeat that some aspects of labor that are very difficult and require great experience, are often completely ignored. Let us take for example the difficult task of a schoolteacher.

The schoolteacher was always unjustly underpaid and always remained under suspicion from all sides. Yet everybody easily understands that the education of his children can be entrusted only to a person who is really educated and who has a basic knowledge of the fundamentals of science. Everybody also understands that such a person must be sufficiently provided for in order not to distract himself by looking for additional, necessary income. No doubt everyone will agree with these primary conditions demanded by life. Yet in public and governmental budgets, the schoolteacher remains as before in pitiful circumstances. More than that, if in the treasury there is a lack of funds, it will be the schoolteacher, the physician, the scientist who will be excluded from the budget in the first order. We do not mention here the writers, artists, and similar independent professions that are most needed for public education, and yet are the least taken care of by the state. Is it not so?

On the basis of all such lamentable misunderstandings, there lies ignorance in appreciation of labor. Only recently, experimental psychologists came to the conclusion that intellectual work uses up three times as much energy as manual labor. Of course, we do not want this statement to belittle any form of labor, but we mention this statement in the cause of justice. Naturally, everyone desires that his country should prosper. Everyone is happy when some public enterprise is extolled. And yet it is only as an exception that people understand the entire real value of labor spent on these achievements. It has been correctly said that "he who does not work has no right to eat." No idlers and parasites have a right to live. Untiringly, one must educate public opinion as to what labor for Common Good really means. *Hélas*, this is not yet a truism!

The many instructive historical examples were given to humanity, not in vain. The great example of the shoemaker, Boehme; or of the manufacturer of lenses, Spinoza; of priests who were master weavers; and finally the illustrious example of the Master carpenter were, it should seem, sufficient to indicate the quality of labor. And we also remember how the great educator of Russia, St. Sergius of Radonega, starved rather than accept a piece of bread unless it was earned by labor.

Such striking and appealing examples should be persuasively taught in all schools. Thereby, an equilibrium in the evaluation of various kinds of labor would be reached. Much vanity would then disappear, but, on the other hand, there would arise a sincere joy at every labor that has been carried out beautifully. If all this is merely a truism, then why is it not applied everywhere?!

Why is that up to now the Ministry of Public Education, Labor, and Agriculture—in other words, everything connected with peaceful prosperity—has been treated as being third- and fourth-rate? And very often such important departments of life are altogether absorbed in some far less peaceful considerations. This is so, and no one can insist that this anguish of the heart is exaggerated.

What has been said is not only true, but it is never sufficiently underlined. One, unfortunately, sees that many people avoid thinking of humanitarian questions, of cultural values, neglect them, and do not place them in the proper place as befits a civilized country. *Hélas*, one sees so often that people reject precisely that which lies at the foundation of peaceful constructiveness. Apostles of Good sternly condemned those ignoramuses, who did not revere the high significance of labor. Such people need not eat; they are not wanted for evolution; they are the scum of the earth. Apostles of Good thus justly censured the criminal neglect of labor. For both in the East and West, it is equally well known that ignorance is the mother of all vices.

Nowadays, during this reign of mechanization, an especially attentive attitude toward labor is required, and justice toward workers in all manifold fields of life is imperative. People have already guessed that mania for robots is not a sign of accomplishment. Thereby, a qualitative creative basis of every labor will be established.

Look and see how true workers are untiringly at their desks. Every day, in diligence and patience, they are not creating for themselves but for the general benefit. In these anonymous efforts and sacrifices is contained a true grandeur. The hieroglyph of labor becomes a collective concept. When one hears "Edison," one thinks no longer of Thomas Edison but of a powerful, collective conception of inventiveness for the benefit of humanity. In the same way, when the names "Raphael or Rubens" are pronounced, they are not so much personal as characteristic of an entire epoch.

On ancient Chinese works of art, there are imprinted certain marks. They also represent nothing personal. They have become as if the seals of their age. May the seal of our age be a broad, just realization of labor. Let no useful creative worker be forgotten. May in all countries the question of education, enlightenment, and labor stand foremost!

UNKNOWN ARTISTS

[*The Theosophist.* Adyar, Vol. LVII, No. 12,
September, 1936, pp. 500–503]

EXHIBITIONS were lately held, demonstrating the idea of which I had already the occasion to write and speak several times. From the point of view of the history of art, it is always most important to reveal the so-called unknown artists. The names of great masters are very often in public judgment collective conceptions. When looking over the standard handbooks on art, we will find, in addition to the well-known celebrities, numerous names whose creations are not commonly known. And yet these artists lived to an old age, worked incessantly, and had as their teachers, great masters.

About an exhibition in Paris, the press reported the following: "An exhibition of sixty paintings, acclaimed by connoisseurs as the highest works of art but bearing the signatures of unknown artists, was organized in Paris under the patronage of Georges Huysmans and was heralded to be the most remarkable of the series of thirty exhibitions of the Parisian season."

An exhibition of unknown artists reminded old collectors and critics of many episodes concerning mistakes of judgment committed by the best authorities on art.

One of them narrates: "Thirty years ago I got the idea of submitting to the jury of an exhibition a small Roman landscape painted in light-yellow and bluish colors, and also a pen drawing representing a peasant with a large hat. Both paintings were flatly refused. And yet the landscape was by Corot, and the drawing was nothing less than one by Rembrandt himself."

Another art critic added that paintings by unknown authors were now and then acquired by the largest art museums and believed to be by known great masters. On a recent exhibition of old Italian art in Paris, there was exhibited the famous *Open-Air Concert*, previously catalogued by outstanding authorities as a Titian and now regarded as a masterpiece of Giorgione.

Such anecdotes remind us of the famous saying of Toulouse-Lautrec: "A painting should be perceived by the heart." In other words, a painting should be valued on its merit, and not because of the signature. This French artist adds: "What would it matter if an image of an Evangelist turns out not to be by Velasquez, if its high-quality ranks it equal to the brush of the latter!"

We can remember many facts from life that prove on what quicksand conventional judgment is based. In the Metropolitan Museum of Art in New York, there is a painting attributed to Matsys that is actually a painting of the very interesting but completely unknown master of the Netherlands, Hasselaer. His signature, which I and the well-known authority on art, Senator Semenoff-Tianshansky, have seen, was evidently removed by its previous owner. On the market, it is, of course, an entirely different thing to sell an unknown Hasselaer in order to have the opportunity to offer a famous Matsys.

I myself have seen a written certificate by a well-known authority stating a painting to be a Rembrandt. Yet from this painting there had just been removed the name of Jan Victors, a distinguished pupil of Rembrandt. I also remember a landscape of the eighteenth century, under which was visible an older signature of the seventeenth century. One may cite many stories that eloquently prove that a painting should be judged not by the signature but on its merit.

There are two types of collectors. One group requires, first of all, only the name. The other demands an artistic quality. For the collectors of the former type, there have been created innumerable fakes. A rather rude art dealer used to laugh: "A signature costs but a couple of shillings!"

Many tragedies and dramas in the art word are due to conventional judgment. Again, if we take the largest encyclopedia on art, one is struck by a multitude of completely unknown names who apparently left no result of their activities, yet they were connected with the greatest masters. They were commissioned to adorn cathedrals and public buildings, which proves that they were *en vogue*. Besides, their names were cited by old historians of art, who obviously had cause to esteem them greatly. Verily, judging by the rare signed painting, one is convinced that these artists, although unknown to us, were great and excellent masters who fully deserved their page in the history of art.

If even today, before our very eyes, there disappears a signature from a painting, then evidently such sinister episodes also took place in the past. It is said about a well-known collector that he always carried with him a vial with alcohol, and while bargaining for a painting, he washed off the signature to decrease the value of the painting. Many tragedies indeed have taken place around art objects. We ourselves were once horrified at seeing how a restorer reduced a beautiful painting to a seemingly dilapidated condition in order to purchase it cheaply.

After all, one can write the most instructive story about the life of paintings and other art objects. Who knows, perhaps some dramatist will someday take as his subject not a human being but the tragedy from the life of a painting. A long procession of dramatic, tragic, and highly joyful and solemn episodes are depicted around the works of art, weaving their aura.

Everyone has heard of the destruction of masterpieces of Leonardo by religious fanatics and cruel invaders. I remember how a beautiful sketch by Rubens was used as cardboard for the binding of a book. An excellent portrait by Bryullov was covered by an ugly landscape. Under the excellent painting attributed to Ingres was discovered the signature of his collaborator, Carbonniere. In all countries, there has always taken place intentional or involuntary shiftings of names and definitions. Together with revaluations and fashions, every century had its own conventionalities. Instead of true revaluation, new concealments are taking place.

But let us not dwell on old art only. The problem of contemporary art is still more acute. May the examples of the past teach our generation to open their hearts to young artists! And after all, who can affirm who are the unknown and the known artists, and to whom are they known or unknown?

I have been told of a most remarkable collection of "unknown" French artists of the recent period. A collector from Marseilles began to collect paintings of artists who died very young or who, in despair, discarded art. A large collection was assembled. A visitor who did not know the names might have thought that they were paintings by Degas, Monet, Manet, Rafaeli, Menard, LaTouche, and other celebrated French artists. This collection also contained some strongly individual conceptions. It became quite clear that at some time, an enterprising person may arrange from such a collection a most striking and significant exhibition. Besides paintings of artists who died early in life, there were those of artists who considered themselves *decouragés*. And it is yet another question whether they were all right considering themselves failures. Sometimes a terrible injustice brings people to this entirely undeserved self-estimate.

A friend of ours when saying "unknown" always used to add "unknown to me." And in this, he was quite right. How can anyone say that a person unknown to him at the moment, and in a certain place, may not be greatly revered by other people elsewhere? Such a consideration should be understood by many people nowadays. Otherwise, in self-conceit, some people may imagine, that if they do not know something or do not accept it, then all other people also do not know and do not admit it. Such is the usual vanity of the ignoramus. Besides, the question of being known or unknown is one of the most conditional. This definition is based on many casual circumstances, both conscious and unconscious. Many excellent geniuses received recognition only after their death. For some curious reasons, people seem to value only the factor of death in their judgments.

Hélas! Because of crass ignorance, so often the ugly *Danse Macabre* replaces the beautiful predestined Dance of Life. May exhibitions of "unknown" artists remind us once more of the conventionality of human judgment, and may they create one more act of justice in the contemporary world.

Shrimati Rukmini Devi, in her inspiring article "The Sense of Beauty" (*The Theosophist*, June 1936), says: "The true end of all art is that each one of us should be artistic, that each one of us should be able to appreciate beauty, to be able to work in harmony with all life, and that the life of each of us must become so refined, so artistic that we shall irresistibly respond to every fine and noble thing."

Verily, in every academy, institute, and school of art, besides the artistic technicalities, there should be instilled the true sense of beauty. The sense of beauty, even if it is inborn, still needs educating for unfoldment. In the same way, though every human being has been given the gift of thought, yet the art of thinking also needs education. The classical Museion—the home of all muses, was precisely that Temple, where the sense of beauty was developed and glorified. In the same manner, people should welcome every upliftment and refining of the human spirit that takes place in such unifying noble temples, reminding us of the glorious academia of ancient Greece. These beautiful hearths were the sign of a true renaissance. In the all-unifying academia, people will learn to become more kind, honest, and just. These qualities also belong to the same great concept of the Beautiful.

IN DEFENCE OF ART

[*The Four Arts Annual.* Calcutta, 1936–1937, pp. 6–7]

"HUMANITY is facing the coming events of cosmic greatness. Humanity already realizes that all occurrences are not accidental. The time for the construction of future culture is at hand. Before our eyes, the revaluation of values is being witnessed. Amid ruins of valueless banknotes, mankind has found the real value of the world's significance. The values of great art are victoriously traversing all storms of earthly commotions. Even the "earthly" people already understand the vital importance of active beauty. And when we proclaim: Love, Beauty, and Action, we know, verily, that we pronounce the formula of the international language. And this formula, which now belongs to the museum and the stage, must enter everyday life. The Sign of Beauty will open all Sacred Gates. Beneath the Sign of Beauty we walk joyfully. With Beauty we conquer. Through Beauty we pray. In Beauty we are united. And now we affirm these words—not on the snowy heights but amid the turmoil of the city. And realizing the path of true reality, we greet with a happy smile, the future."

Thus, we addressed cultural units fifteen years ago. And still earlier, thirty years ago, we sent out our first plea for the protection of cultural treasures. And these three decades not only did not lessen the imperativeness of this call but many ineffaceably tragic events have since proved the undeferrability of this S.O.S. During these three decades has the safety of artistic and scientific values been affirmed? On the contrary, the planet has witnessed horrible vandalism that leaves, in the history of humanity, a most deplorable page. Many phases of life have been hastened during these decades; but has the veneration for the artist, the scientist, and other cultural workers increased?

Has the life of the young artist become less burdensome? Has public opinion, amid the many disputes and discussions about prices in the domain of art, learned to appreciate the real value of artistic creations? If the public opinion of all countries would have come to the defense of art and science, we would not hear of those cruelties and vandalisms that fill the newspapers today.

If the monuments of art and science are testimonies to the level of national dignity, then the public opinion of the entire world should stand on vigil in order that these unique treasures may not be violated. If from the remotest ages we hear of horrible destructions, now that mankind pretends that it has become more civilized, how much more reason there is to see that such gloomy pages of history should under no circumstances be repeated? All cultural and ethical strivings should be directed to prevent such atrocities from occurring again. Evolution is not senseless destruction but constructiveness in the widest sense of this concept.

It is sad to receive from everywhere expressions of horror and despair. Only yesterday, we had the occasion to write to a friend in distress:

You write about the Banner of Peace:

"What is the use of it when you have to deal with savages—with people who do not respect their own signature and who cannot trust or be trusted?" It is strange how this reminds one of the similar questions made over half a century ago at the time when the noble Dunant promulgated the great idea of the Red Cross. As you know, this panhuman ideal took over seventeen years until realized universally. While beginning our movement, we, of course, studied the history of the Red Cross and met with much scoffing, negation, and ridicule; yet the benevolent humanitarian idea has triumphed, and no one will say today that the idea of the Red Cross is useless. You write that the idea of protection of cultural treasures is a vague one. From our entire activity, you know that by nature we are against every form of vagueness and uncertainty. I know, thoroughly, the value of introducing into life a firm stimulus for the defense of human dignity, and, as an educator, I can affirm that students from young years were most anxious to guard their national treasures. Without any vagueness, these constructive principles should be upheld. The question of preservation of treasures of art and science remains indisputable. I fully understand the nervous tone of your letter; for when we are facing brutal destructions, one cannot remain unperturbed, and especially such a sensitive lover and connoisseur of art as you must become indignant. Already since 1903, I have been ardently working for the defense of art and science, and no amount of skepticism and scoffing can convince me that this work is not necessary. And the more brutal circumstances become, the more imperative is every effort to preserve the best treasures of humanity. Already, twenty-one countries have signed the Pact of the Banner of Peace.

How many similar calls one has to send out into space! And in all these discussions, it becomes clear that the main distress and error lie in the fact that the real cultural forces are widely scattered and do not find a common meeting ground on which they could powerfully and unitedly affirm their righteous judgment. Everyone in his own sphere can help. Everyone can speak to the younger generation about their beautiful duty.

The heart of the woman, in all its vigilance and sensitiveness, can from every hearth send a message in defense of the most sacred treasures of the human spirit.

Innumerable are the ways of affirmation of culture; and it is especially dear to me to pronounce these words in a country where since the ancient times of the *Rigveda*, the most magnificent ordainments of Beauty and Wisdom were manifested.

Help at every hour of the day! Help in all your labors! Help from the depth of your heart—for without love there can be no help. In helping the smallest, you venerate the Highest.

"On all paths to Me, I shall meet thee!"

Help! Help! Help!

GLORY TO PUSHKIN, THE GREATEST RUSSIAN POET

On the Occasion of the Centenary of his Death

[*The New Outlook* Vol. III, No. 2, March, 1937, pp. 125–128]

ON February 10th, 1837, the greatest Russian poet, Pushkin, died after receiving a fatal wound in a duel. The name of Pushkin is known all over the world. The sad centenary of his violent death was reverenced in the whole world by all true lovers of literature. Not only in the immense vastness of Russia but in all countries, there were held solemn celebrations; exhibitions were opened dedicated to the poet, and many new editions of his famous works were published. In Russian and European theatres, his immortal dramas were produced in the musical interpretation of the best Russian composers.

The commemorative event resulted in a great Day of Russian or, rather, world culture. The immortal creations of Pushkin, equal to Shakespeare, Dante, Goethe, and Balzac, will forever remain a vital, inexhaustible source of spiritual enrichment of the present and future generations of humanity. *Eugene Onegin*, *Poltava*, *The Bronze Rider*, *The Captain's Daughter*, *Ruslan and Ludmila*, *The Queen of Spades*, and hundreds of other works of Pushkin will live as precious evidence of radiant thought, as expressions of the feelings of true, noble inspiration.

Pushkin's poems, written over a hundred years ago, move the hearts of mankind as deeply now as they did at the time of his contemporaries. Only now has the glory of Pushkin become a truly universal glory.

He has expressed the inner life of the country in unprecedented, evoking artistic images. For Pushkin the poet, there were no geographical nor historical boundaries. Ancient Hellas, Rome, Italy, Spain, the ancient and new East, and all Slavonic thoughts were reflected by him with the same deep comprehension.

No one has before or after Pushkin enriched Russian culture to such an extent as this greatest poet of his motherland. He was the true creator of the Russian literary language. He has conquered for Russian literature a place of honor in world classics. The poems, stories, and essays of Pushkin prove the inexhaustible wealth of human expressions. Pushkin was the creator of a magnificent, flexible, expressive Russian literary language. He imbued Russian literature with the spirit of the people; he magnified the language with innumerable words taken from the very depths of folklore treasury. He introduced real poetical gems of national bards. Pushkin's contemporaries used to say about him that he was ever restless, that his spirit was rebellious, and, as such, he died.

The great Russian critic, Belinsky, thus defined Pushkin's poetry: "What a style! Antique plasticity and stern simplicity were combined in him with the charming play of romantic rhythm. The entire acoustic wealth, the might of the Russian language were revealed in him in extraordinary perfection; he is delicate, sweet, tender, like the murmur of the waves; he is rich as soil, brilliant as lightning, transparent and pure as crystal, aromatic and fragrant as spring, strong and mighty as the sword in the hand of a hero. Should we want to describe the verse of Pushkin in one word, we would say that it is *par excellence*, a truly poetic, artful, and artistic verse; and this would solve the mystery of the majestic pathos of the entire poetry of Pushkin."

Gorky, usually severe in his judgment, says of Pushkin: "Pushkin is for Russian literature what Leonardo da Vinci was for European art. We have before us a great Russian national poet, the creator of poetical tales, who charms with their beauty and wit; the author of the first realistic novel, *Eugene Onegin*; the author of our best historical drama, *Boris Godunov*; a poet who, up until now, is unsurpassed in the beauty of his verse and in the mighty expressions of emotions and thoughts; a poet—the father of great Russian literature. In the person of Pushkin, we have the example of a writer who, being imbued with impressions of life, was striving to reflect them in verse and prose with the greatest truth, with utmost realism, and in this, he succeeded as a real genius. His creations are a most valuable testimony of a clever, wise, truthful person about customs, habits, and conceptions of a certain period—indeed they are the true records of Russian history by a genius."

As befits every great man, Pushkin suffered great injustice from his contemporaries. The great poet was exiled, and for a long time there hung upon him the threat of evil suspicions. This cannot be avoided—without these torchers of savages, no great achievement is possible. Thanks to his all-containing heart, Pushkin joined all advanced movements and was a friend of free thought. We find him amongst the *Decabrists*. We see Pushkin as a mason, and to this society belonged all the foremost thinkers of Russia. The poet was seeking everywhere for Truth; and listening to the fairy tales of his old nurse, he was enchanted from his very childhood by the beauty of Russian folklore.

During the short span of his life (1799–1837), while studying historical chronicles, he yet remained ever in the defense of the new, carrying in his heart the vision of Russia's great future. When still in the Lyceum, Pushkin already astonished everyone with his sonorous verse, and the great Derzhavin blessed him and foretold his glory. Seldom can one's heart embrace simultaneously both the East and West. Every reader in the Orient will understand Pushkin's *Ruslan and Ludmila, The Captive of the Caucasus,* or *The Fountain of Bakhchisarai.* Whereas *Eugene Onegin, The Queen of Spades,* or *Dubrovsky* will resound in Western hearts.

Boris Godunov, the drama in which Pushkin, with astounding depth, unfolds the tragedy of a ruler "who has attained the highest power," now attracts the attention of the whole world. Recently, *Boris Godunov* was staged in Berlin; in Praha—*Eugene Onegin.* Thus, in the most diverse and even contradictory audiences, the splendor of Pushkin's creations calls forth equal admiration.

As we see, Pushkin simultaneously proceeded by all creative paths. During the twenty-seven years of his literary career, Pushkin became a great poet, a great prosaist, and a great dramatist. In his works we have examples of all literary styles. Every new creation of Pushkin was not only a real *chef-d'oeuvre* but became a new chapter in the history of Russian literature. In his immeasurable artistic might, in his extraordinary multifacetedness, in his unusual alacrity of mind are expressed the potentiality and genius of the great nation in which he was born. Let us remember his Self-characteristic poems "Echo" and "The Prophet," which are significant as describing the view of the poet upon his mission in life. Let us not attempt to translate them into poetical verse, but try to render the poet's thought:

Echo

> Whether beasts roar in forests deep—
> Whether the horn sounds or thunders storm,
> Whether a maiden sings on hillocks far—
> To every voice
> An echo in the empty air
> Resounds at once.

> Thou heedest to the thunder's roar,
> The calls of storm and waves,
> To shouts of shepherds
> You an answer send,
> But you get no response. . . .
> This, poet, is your fate!

In the other poem "Prophet," a six-winged Seraphim appears on the crossroad to a wanderer and, touching his lips and ears, opens to him his prophetic vision. The tremors of heaven and mysteries of earth and sea are revealed to him. The Seraphim tears out his tongue and replaces it with the wisdom of the serpent; for his heart, he substitutes a piece of glowing coal. The poem concludes as follows:

> Alone as lifeless corpse in deserts I remained,
> And God's voice called:
> Arise, thou prophet, behold and hearken!
> Be filled with My glory,
> And, faring seas and distant lands,
> By word the hearts of men thou set aflame!

Thus, the poet foresaw his glorious mission.

CULTURAL UNITY OF NATIONS

[*The Educational Review.* Madras, Vol. XLIV, No. 1,
January, 1938, pp. 1-3]

OUR times are verily difficult because of all the commotions of the spirit, all nonunderstanding, and all attacks of darkness against Light. Quite recently there were pictures in magazines showing the *auto-da-fé* of precious books in the streets. It is hard to realize that this could have taken place in the present age, after millions of years of the existence of our planet. But perhaps this terrible tension is the impulse to direct humanity through all storms and over all abysses to peaceful construction and mutual respect.

What an epoch-making day might be before us when over all countries, all centers of spirit, beauty, and knowledge could be unfurled the one Banner of Culture! This sign would call everyone to revere the treasures of human genius, to respect culture, and to have a new valuation of labor as the only measure of true values. From childhood, people will witness that there exists not only a flag for human health, but there is also a sign of peace and culture for the health of the spirit. This sign, unfurled over all treasures of human genius, will say: "Here are guarded the treasures of all mankind; here, above all petty divisions, above illusory frontiers of enmity and hatred is towering the fiery stronghold of love, labor, and all-moving creation."

Real peace is desired by the human heart. It strives to labor creatively and actively. For its labor is a source of joy. It wants to love and expand in the realization of Sublime Beauty. In the highest perception of Beauty and Knowledge, all conventional divisions disappear. The heart speaks its own language; it wants to rejoice in that which is common for all, uplifts all, and leads to the radiant Future. All symbols and tablets of humanity contain one hieroglyph, the sacred prayer—Peace.

It is truly beautiful if amid the turmoil of life, in the waves of unsolved social problems, we still may hold up before us the eternal Flambeaux (torches) of Peace in all ages. It is beautiful, through the inexhaustible well of love and tolerance, to understand the great movements that connected the highest knowledge with the highest aspirations. Thus, in studying and admiring, we are becoming real cooperators with evolution, and out of the brilliant rays of Supreme Light may emerge true knowledge. This refined knowledge is based on real comprehension and tolerance. From this source comes the great understanding, rises the supremely Beautiful, the enlightening and refining enthusiasm for Peace. Contemporary life is changing rapidly; the signs of a new evolution are knocking at all doors. In real unconventional science, we feel the splendid responsibility before the coming generations. We understand gradually the harm of everything negative. We begin to value enlightened positiveness and constructiveness, and in this measure, in merciful tolerance, we can prepare for our next generation a vital happiness, turning vague abstractions into beneficent realities.

On the scrolls of command, it has been inscribed that a spiritual garden is daily in need of the same watering as a garden of flowers. If we still consider the physical flowers the true adornment of our life, then how much more must we remember and prescribe to the creative values of the spirit of the leading place in the life that surrounds us? Let us, then, with untiring, eternal vigilance, benevolently mark the manifestations of the workers of culture; and let us strive in every possible way to ease this difficult path of heroic achievement.

Let us also mark and find a place in our lives for the Great Ones, remembering that their name no longer is personal, with all the attributes of the limited ego, but has become the property of panhuman cultures and must be safeguarded and firmly cared for in most benevolent conditions.

We shall thus continue their self-sacrificing labor and we shall cultivate their creative sowing, which, as we see, is so often covered with the dirt of non-understanding and overgrown with the weeds of ignorance.

As a caring gardener, the true culture bearer will not forcefully crush those flowers that entered life not from the main road if they belonged to the same precious kinds that he safeguards. The manifestations of culture are just as manifold as are the manifestations of the endless varieties of life itself. They ennoble Be-ness. They are the true branches of the one sacred Tree, whose roots sustain the Universe.

If you shall be asked of what kind of country and of what a future constitution you dream, you can answer in full dignity: "We visualize the country of Great Culture." The country of Great Culture will be your noble motto. You shall know that in that country will be peace, where Knowledge and Beauty will be revered.

Everything created by hostility is impractical and perishable. The history of mankind gave us remarkable examples of how necessary peaceful creativeness was for progress. The hand will tire from the sword, but the creating hand, sustained by the might of the Spirit, is untiring and unconquerable. No sword can destroy the heritage of Culture. The human mind may temporarily deviate from the primary courses, but at the predestined hour will have to recur to them with the renovated powers of the spirit.

Culture and Peace make man verily invincible, and realizing all spiritual conditions, he becomes tolerant and all-embracing. Each intolerance is but a sign of weakness. If we understand that every lie, every fallacy shall be exposed, it means that, first of all, a lie is stupid and impractical. But what has he to hide who has consecrated himself to Peace and Culture? Helping his near, he helps the general welfare that at all ages was appreciated. Striving to Peace, he becomes a pillar of a progressing State. Not slandering the near, we increase the productiveness of the common creativeness. Not quarreling we shall prove that we possess the knowledge of the foundations. Not wasting time in idleness, we shall prove that we are true coworkers in the ploughfield of Culture. Finding joy in everyday labor, we show that the conception of Infinity is not alien to us. Not harming others, we do not harm ourselves; and eternally giving, we realize that in giving we receive. And this blessed receiving is not a hidden treasure of a miser. We understand how creative is affirmation and how destructive is negation. Amid basic conceptions, those of Peace and Culture are the conceptions that even a complete ignoramus will not dare to attack. There where is Culture, is Peace. There, where is the right solution for the difficult social problems is achievement. Culture is the cumulation of the highest Bliss, of highest Beauty, of highest Knowledge.

We are tired of destructions and negations. Positive creativeness is the fundamental quality of the human spirit. Let us welcome all those who, surmounting personal difficulties and casting aside petty selfishness, propel their spirits to the task of preserving Culture, thus insuring a radiant future. We must not fear enthusiasm. Only the ignorant and the spiritually impotent would scoff at this noble feeling. Such scoffing is but the sign of inspiration for the true Legion of Honor. Nothing can impede us from dedicating ourselves to the service of Culture as long as we believe in it and give to it our most flaming thoughts.

Do not disparage! The great Agni singes the drooping wings. Only in harmony with evolution can we ascend! And nothing can extinguish the selfless and flaming wings of enthusiasm!

HEARKEN AND HASTEN!

[*Peace.* Godavari, No. 1, January–February, 1938, pp. 18–19]

THE concept of a Federation contains the ideals of work, knowledge, action, and cooperation. All these fundamentals constitute the cooperative movement that is at present so much appreciated and acclaimed all over the world.

Indeed, humanity is in need not of abstract ideas but real constructiveness. It would be a mistake to suppose that the cooperative movement is only applicable to industry or agriculture. This vital movement can enter and imbue every branch of human life. Even in early school years and throughout all specializations of life, this method is possible and should be studied.

Whatever faculty of a university we may take, be it philosophy, medicine, law, economics, natural science, physics, etc., everywhere can be created units on a cooperative basis. Further on, these units can be assembled into larger organizations, vitally assisting each other. Especially now when the question of unemployment everywhere has become so acute, one should develop such self-activity.

Successful examples of such beneficial work are evident in many countries and various fields of life. Also, in India I had an opportunity to witness, in several places, the welfare that had resulted from such beginnings. In these cooperative societies, both science and art can have their place of honor. The love for the book can be reaffirmed and art can enter all homes, for indeed knowledge and beauty are for the people.

Such self-activity saves people from prejudice and fear—these terrifying and paralyzing monsters. True science will help to cognize the visible and the unseen. People will thus understand how to realize the protection of cultural treasures that belong, beyond all earthly boundaries, to the entire humanity. On the fields of the cooperative movement will grow the beautiful flowers of Culture and Peace.

The infinite might of Culture may well be expressed in the following historical narrative:

"The Great Akbar once drew a line and demanded of Birbal the Wise that he shorten the line without cutting and erasing from either end. The latter drew a longer line parallel to it, and Akbar's line was thereby shortened. Wisdom lies in drawing the longer line."

I wish you, my dear young friends, to cherish in your hearts the lofty wisdom of your Great *Bharat Mata*. I wish you the achievement of the longest beautiful line in your creative united labors!

ON SACRED VIGIL

Greetings to the Boy Scouts of India

[*The Culture.* India, 1938]

IT gives me much pleasure to respond to your request and to send this heartfelt message to the glorious Association of Boy Scouts in India. To greet the Boy Scouts means to hail the young generation in which lies our hope for Progress, Friendship, and Peace. The Boy Scouts are the guard of honor for their Motherland. They are guardians of Beauty and Knowledge. Precisely the young generations must understand their duty in upholding the fundamental concepts of life—Art and Knowledge, on which evolution rests.

The Boy Scouts and Girl Guides are always prepared to defend everything noble and humanitarian. When we unfurled our Banner of Peace, we had in view, first of all, the young generation that understands its duty in defending the real treasures of humanity. From the first school years, the Boy Scouts already know that the renaissance of the nation comes from Art and Science in its highest form.

Youth know that spiritual aspirations are the guidance to lofty Heights. More than once humanity deplored atrocities and vandalism. Precisely the young knights should be prepared to defend untiringly the great heroic achievements that have been created by the best of mankind for the common benefit. The Boy Scouts and Girl Guides know the meaning of discipline. They are concerned also with sports and physical training, with the object of the general betterment of life. Service, Self-sacrifice, Honor, Friendship, Vigil,

Courage, and joyful Labor—all these noble virtues are inseparable from the concept of Scoutism. We have proclaimed *Pax Per Cultura*—indeed, real peace is only there where is true Culture.

In the name of these foundations of progress, I am sending my ardent greetings and wishes for heroic success.

URBANISM

[*The Scholar.* Palghat, Vol. XIII, No. 6,
March, 1938, pp. 324–328]

IN all the changes of names can be read the history of civilization. At one time certain people were called *burghers*, that is, those who collected around the burg, the castle. Under the protection of its walls and towers arose the growth of the concept of townspeople. The townsman, the burgess, was likewise identified with some city, some fortified place. Gradually with the decline of the feudal structure, the concept of *burgherhood* also became outworn. For a long time, it remained as a purely conventional designation, having lost its inner, formerly very definitive, meaning.

At the changing of outworn concepts and designations, many new ones grow up. At times they continue as it were and develop further the former concept, but sometimes the resulting extermination advances a definition just as outwardly conventional as the latest survivals. In most recent times, the word *urbanism* is employed in different countries around the concept of the city. There is something very vague in this derivative from the Latin word *urbs*. The city, the Latin *urbs*, generally appears as an indefinite concept. An assembly of people form such a populous locale, and you do not distinguish whether such a place is a fortress, a commercial center, a cultural center, or its usual principal form containing all sorts of bazaars. Yet at the same time, such a peculiarly, singularly definitive will be in the word *urbanism*.

Urbanism somehow characterizes those frigid city agglomerations that have made poisonously, unhealthy places in these crowded myriads of people. Even in those cities whereby a fortunate accident there have not risen accumulations—even right now there are people who are trying to heap up structures in the name of some strange modernism. There can be recited a whole list of cities that, without any visible need, are killing all the already composed character of the place and are making haste to install some enormous edifices, precisely as if there was not far more than enough space in the country.

There have appeared some sort of artist *urbanists*, architect *urbanists*, technician *urbanists*. In many of its applications, the concept of *urbanism*, like the recently invented technocracy, has appeared rather intrusive. In this deliberate intrusiveness, there always proves to be something premeditated, some premature senility. Not for long did technocracy flourish. Not even the monkey glands of Voronov could help it. Likewise, precisely urbanism, in its intrusive self-assurance, does not suspect its own short-livedness in the aspect in which it is understood at present.

There may be some against the urban structure. Many thoughts have been devoted to solving the city problem. City gardens would not be urbanism, which would like to place itself in exact opposition to life in the country. No society can successfully solve its vital problems on a foundation of decadent superstitions and fossilized horrors. Likewise, precisely in the problem of the city, it is impossible to think only about ancient Babylonian towers. This Biblical symbol would seem to emphasize sufficiently the limits of uniform thinking. Any decadence, either material or spiritual, is identically worthless.

In place of the Babylonian towering piles, humanity is again beginning to remember about returning to nature. Even not so long ago, ill-considered measures dragged farmers away from their fields and rounded up starving crowds in unemployment in the city. Right now, one can understand the terror of these enormous throngs of people that are ending up in misanthropy. Again, thoughts have arisen about a return to natural work that, through the contemporary discoveries of science, can be transformed into a fuller life, both spiritually and materially.

Everywhere are appearing individual persons, families, and entire groups of people who dream about a life in the middle of nature. Both on small and large scales, they are thinking up all sorts of cooperatives that, in varied work, would enable them to lead a working life that is natural, full, and sensible. One can only rejoice if the latest contemporary discoveries and social movements can lead people to thoughts about nature, about natural improvements in the different applications of labor.

The loss of the city symbols and the arrival at the coldly conventional urbanism is, as it were, the entryway to new and vital labor structures. Again, the human spirit must rush back to nature in which there is so much free space and unused and unrealized possibilities. To the same thoughts about nature and to the various improvements in the matter of health, refer the tasks of making the deserts bloom. By wise, undeferrable measures let these spaces neglected by the carelessness of people be made again fruitful and useful for habitation.

Many thoughts are narrated regarding the best methods of agriculture, forestry, and other conditions relating to rural life. Not long ago, V. N. Mehta, in an Indian journal, properly remarked about the rehabilitation of rural life. He says, "Many physicians are working on the treatment of illness when it happens to the small villager. They have found that he has gone into debt, and the indebtedness forces him, as it were, into the hospital. But such endless detention in an infirmary cannot be recognized as a remedy in practical usage, and, consequently, many recipes are filling space—the more quickly to release such a patient from the hospital, and furnish him with a reasonable period for convalescence."

Further on, the author comes to the conclusion: "The small villager should not be fed on falsehood. Let him be given the inner impulse to set his affairs to right. Do not urbanize him. In that case, of course, he suffers the fate that the French beautifully express by the word *déraciné*—torn away, uprooted, a spectacle worthy of regret and requiring special considerations from each reformer. There can be observed two streams rushing out of the same watershed that, at last, flow together in the Ganges Felix. These streams must enrich the soil over which they pass and, in their course, bring regeneration to the countryside. Make no mistake about it. The peasantry must be so reorganized that it can augment threefold its economic level and its spiritual growth."

Indeed, this Hindu writer could not but end his just considerations with one precisely about spiritual growth. In each new settlement, in each abode in the midst of nature, the question of spirituality must enter more strongly into all of life. The entire way of life in nature cannot be limited by any technocracy. Many beautiful and vital thoughts will drift together at the closest contact with nature, in the blessed everyday labors. Calling these labors blessed is no exaggeration of their significance because to them can be easily attached all the best self-cultivation. Radio, television, and all paths of facilitated communication—of course, these are not for urbanism—all these beneficial possibilities are required precisely in the broad expanse of nature, among the again blossoming meadows and filled granaries.

The definition, *urbanism*, in its boldness, was probably predestined for cutting short in time the harmfulness of the sickened and poisoned life in the city. It would be extremely deplorable if there should not be immediately opposed to these maladies the garden dwellings in which will be combined the best individualities with rich opportunities for collaboration, cooperation. One comes to an end in order for the other to prosper, in eternal life. Throughout the broad horizon, there are no obstacles, no city monstrosities, and no Babylonian towers to overshadow the paths to the flowering garden of nature. During the last year, the idea of Urbanism received some terrible blows. If the urbanists would summarize the number of destroyed houses by air raids and shelling, they would get monstrous totals. Even from casual newspaper data, one can see the ever-growing number of destructions even when war, as such, has not been declared. In one of my *Diary Leaves*, mention was made about the "rain of stones." Such a Biblical warning may seem very mild in comparison with a rain of bombs, filled not only with explosives but also with poisonous gases and liquid fire. This is the kind of triumph that *civilization* offers to humanity. What shame!

Recently, people even in Southern Europe were amazed by an unprecedented enormous Aurora Borealis. Thus, the Northern Lights flashed as far down as the South. These magnetic phenomena interfered with radio transmission—thus cosmic energies again entered into human inventions. Let us hope that some kind of *Aurora Universalis* may manifest itself to crush all bombs, shells, poison gases, and other "fratricidal implements of civilization."

SCHOOLS

[*The Scholar*. Palghat, Vol. XIII, No. 9,
June, 1938, pp. 455–459]

CULTURE represents a synthesis of learning, general education, and inborn abilities. Not only the book but the inner level of the family and teacher are the factors that form the world outlook of the youth. Someone or something opens the Gates to the Future. Everyone can remember from childhood moments of exaltation when suddenly the heart was set atremor with inner realization. A beautiful unforgettable moment! In the depths of consciousness, there is retained forever the gratitude to the teacher or to the revealing circumstance. These thoughts will create the beginning of cooperation—the radiant foundation of progress.

Schools, cooperation, and an open eye to new achievements are the Gates to the Future; friends of this or that school may also be of great usefulness. While teachers and parents will be to a certain extent subjective, these friends of the school can always bring to it something new and unexpectedly useful. Besides, the students themselves would often like to listen and exchange thoughts with some new individual outside those making up their daily routine. Strange as it is, often the word of a well-wisher will be listened to with even greater attention than the advice of the everyday teacher. This is one reason why for friends of the school, work can be of an especial advantage.

Likewise, in the formation of all useful, cooperative

institutions, there will pervade a wholesome growth of educational work. I recall how we rejoiced when in the Latvian Society was set forth the idea of a cooperative bakery in the interest of good health. I bring up this example precisely for the reason that I have often had to listen to the surprising question, "What relationship can a bakery have with art and science?" Then I have, again, been obliged to remind about the relationship between bodily and spiritual bread. The late president of the Latvian Society, Doctor F. Lukin, an unforgettable friend and coworker, appreciated full well such combinations that are unexpected for certain people. If we say that science and art are for all life, then also all life, in its lofty quality, will be for science, for creativeness, for beauty, and for all that is the Highest.

Separate friendly guilds and cooperatives can only strengthen the understanding of the unity of the creative principle. On the one hand, people will gather together for conversations and lectures and various manifestations of art. This is certainly needed. It exercises and sharpens thinking and welds people together in friendly agreements. But in addition, any joint work is also useful, illuminated with the same lofty concepts.

At one time in the School of the Society for the Advancement of Arts in Russia, among the two thousand students, over half of the children were of the working class as well as workers themselves from different factories. From this, a noteworthy result was disclosed. All these working people, by manifesting in the factory the new data obtained in our free school, drew the most attention to themselves and secured the best jobs. Thus, we had still another clear example of how much the instruction obtained immediately contributed to receiving higher and more responsible work.

Besides the various classes in applied arts and crafts, all these working people remained in close communication with the examples of beauty in the Museum of the Society, and seeing these earlier attainments, uplifted and refined their consciousness.

Such a reaction to the examples of art should especially, at this time, be strongly mentioned. Perhaps one has had the occasion to hear people ask—even those who have passed through the higher educational institutions—what is the need for the existence of Museums in the presence of such a great number of unemployed? Indeed, such an opinion would show a complete ignorance of methods of education. Of course, unemployment, so aggravated just now, results primarily from insufficient or defective education. This means that all educational societies must be more active in order to eradicate such opinions arising out of ignorance. It should be considered why these higher educational institutions, which strive only to narrow specialization, do not give a broad view of the paths of education. Can schools possibly exist without libraries, museums, laboratories, without all those things that irreplaceably point to the higher forms of reality?

It may seem strange to some that one is obliged, just now, to speak about the utility of material examples. But life unexpectedly gives deplorable indications that show the necessity of these affirmations, even for people who have completed the higher educational courses.

We have always encouraged lectures and classes in the museum rooms themselves and the laboratories. The very atmosphere of these sanctuaries, filled with models and examples, already intensifies the consciousness. Throughout life, we have not been adherents of the abstract. On the contrary, everything vital, everything applicable, has been able to arouse a true joy of realization. All societies must also be directed to the same vitality. They should not be limited to a narrow program. Each country, each society, all forms of education, evoke particular possibilities. If in one place they will be concerned about a bakery, then in another they may wish to have a press, bookshop, or some other completely unexpected synthesized form of work applicable to life.

We have already had exhibitions in hospitals, in prisons, in schools. Continually, the most touching inquiries have been made as a result of these exhibitions. From this can be seen how much the popular consciousness needs and strives for enlightening food. Only let it be given with goodwill easily, freely, in full mutual respect and sympathy. All such useful beginnings can be carried out in any scope whatever. Chiefly they require, first of all, goodwill, needing no particular expenditures. Nowadays, this last circumstance has a special significance. The world, shaken by the moral and material crises at present, often neglects educational necessities. Therefore, educators are compelled, first of all, to think about ways and means not requiring special outlays.

On these good paths, so much true and joyous usefulness can be created by all who generously and smilingly share their experience. Again, let us not think that since libraries, museums, theatres, and laboratories exist, this means these matters have been attended to in sufficient measure. All this exists as ready material that must be brought into popular understanding in the most beautiful and useful form.

Exploratory expeditions traverse a country by one path. But this still does not mean that this whole domain has already been investigated. A thread of cognition has been cut, but the whole broad expanse has still not been explored. Likewise, precisely the various scientific and artistic manifestations in the population enlighten only one stratum of the people, yet so much remains unattained. If even among comparatively educated people you can encounter signs of absolute ignorance, then all sorts of remote settlements are truly deprived of vitalizing knowledge. Look upon their pastimes, upon what fills their leisure time, and you apprehend how undeferrably needed is the bringing of useful knowledge. Good coworkers must untiringly enter into all the strata of life and, with great patience, introduce the life-giving truths.

Every cultural institution, whether large or small, can form groups of devoted workers who, besides mutual meetings and self-education, will undertake visitations to all places where they can bring refreshing usefulness. All these organizations are not made for an egocentric purpose; on the contrary, they must serve only as a possibility for countless new branches.

How joyful can be the meetings of such coworkers—when each one can recount where he has succeeded in bringing something useful. No crises can prevent this useful information. So many enlightening possibilities can be whispered to people who, perhaps through ignorance, are already on the brink of despair.

When the institutions of various countries are in cooperation, what an excellent exchange of possibilities can be established. Where there is patience, there can be no defeats in the lofty tasks. Where there is courage, there are no locked gates. Thus, in the years of crisis, let us speak about what is available for all constructive plans. If everyone everywhere were well and secure, there would be no need for those S.O.S. calls, these lifeboats in all directions. Let no one think that this would be within the limits of arrogance if he desires to bring to the general use the experience that he has gained. This is not pride but a sacred obligation. Surely, it is permitted to no one to be a miser and to bury his silver in the earth for it to become blackened there. As they say in the East, "From buried silver, thy face also will become blackened." Let each one in good cooperation, in true altruism for those around him, enlighteningly make better everything possible. Let him take no thought about whether the matter be large or small, but let it be useful. To bring the useful is each one's obligation. At all times, those who desired the good have been cast into prison—defamed and slandered in every possible way. Yet as a lofty sign of the good, they even came out of their bonds strengthened and radiant. Precisely these stigmata imposed on them by ignoramuses would be manifested as a sign of honor and creativeness of good. It would be a truism to repeat about the usefulness of obstacles, but let us not cease to confirm this ancient truth again and again. Those of our friends who will strive to carry broadly useful knowledge will assuredly encounter many obstacles; it cannot be otherwise. But precisely, then, they will call to mind clearly and enlightenedly the Covenant, "Blessed are the obstacles—by them we grow." And grow they will for the true enlightenment of people. Among all beginnings, pay especial and urgent attention to schools and cooperatives. Essentially, they will both be the banner of true progress.

SOWERS

[*The Educational Review.* Madras, October, 1938]

IN the midst of the desert uplands of Mongolia, where a single tree has not yet been seen, by some miracle there has remained an elm—in the Turkestan language, *Karagatch.* Whether it has been preserved because it has been hidden in a ravine, or that it has lived near a pluvial basin, still it has survived. Whoever are the evil people who have sawed and broken some branches, nevertheless, they have not dared to fell the whole tree. Sometimes, even in the case of hardhearted people, no hand is raised to do something irreparable.

Not only has the elm survived here as the only remaining tree of the former forests, but also it has been occupied with a useful activity—scattering and sowing the slopes surrounding it with young offspring. If no landslide occurs here, if the cruel hand of a destroyer does not come, or if there comes not the cruel hand of a destroyer, then in the future, there will appear an entire grove of elms. Thus, unwearyingly toils the tree—striving in the desolated soil again to create life.

In the vicinity, one can find the stumps and roots of the former forest. Indeed, not nature but the ignorant cruelty of people obtained satisfaction from these guardians of life. Granted that trees are not available beyond a certain altitude when their life-giving property has already been systematically replaced by the quality of mountain Prana. But lower than these heights, let no cruel hand be uplifted in exterminating any life. Let the consciousness be forever impressed by all the life-givers and life-preservers.

You write that time is insufficient for replying to all your diverse correspondence. You write that two hands are not enough to handle all that must be looked after in the course of the day. Remember about this elm, which has held out amid a variety of dangers and, notwithstanding all this, continued the good work of the sower. Gazing at the sawed- and broken-off lower branches, one can picture to oneself how many times an evil-intentioned hand has approached the tree for the purpose of either exterminating it or at least injuring it.

But for all that, in place of destruction, there has taken place the sowing of an entire cluster of young elms. If the tree, in spite of everything, can continue the beneficent labor, then the more can people not be disillusioned and frightened away by any ugly masks. I am very glad to hear that you have too little time. When there is only a little time it becomes precious, and be assured it suffices for everything. Only those who are doing nothing have a lot of time.

If each of us, even for an hour, would have the experience of having nothing to do and of not thinking about anything, then, of course, this would already be the hour of departing from life. In doing, in creating, in the labor of thought, you also remain young and have enough for everything useful. Likewise, picture to yourselves that if by some means you should be deprived of the possibility of continual doing, surely you could no longer survive. Work is a life-giver, and should it cease, here would be true misfortune! The organism, already aspiring to work, would be immediately dissolved under the fetid blast of idleness.

Work, continuous doing, creating is the best tonic remedy. In this panacea will not be included any narcotics, no intoxication is admissible, but the same clear joy will be the source of a long, fruitful life.

Perhaps someone, if you speak to him about your being overly busy, will feel sorry for you. Such condolence will be only through ignorance. Indeed, let us always rejoice at each doer, each creator, each sower. Even if the ploughmen and sowers excite someone's rivalry and envious indignation, this will be only one more stimulus of useful labor. A Marathon of creativeness! A Marathon of work!

You write that people are amazed at how much has been done in such a short period. Tell them that this occurs for the reason that very little time is required to eat your two carrots, as you say, and, in place of inaction, to plunge again into the work that makes you rejoice. Without it, you could not live.

Any work of enlightenment must be first of all joyful. In one sector of labor, there is noted some temporary obstacles; yet you know that in the whole circle of work, there is a vast multitude of sectors. Therefore, do not lament on the *Babylonian rivers*; not from sittings but from vigorous positive creative labor, life flourishes.

Though, as you write, it is difficult for you to succeed in replying to all the various letters; nevertheless, you will find in yourself the means of not leaving these writers in ignorance and of not creating an impression of indifferent aloofness. Many examples might be brought to your attention of how precisely, extremely busy people have always replied immediately to letters. They could not let the matter go because, otherwise, the dams would burst from the heaped-up pressure. Recalling about the iron discipline of labor, we are reminded of Balzac, or those profuse creators of literature, who decidedly found time for everything. Let us not forget that Richelieu, among a multitude of labors, wrote many long discourses and dramas. Let us remember the colossal work that Lomonosov is succeeding in doing! There are not a few such examples.

Let there forever remain as distinguishing marks of all cultural endeavors, love for the work, striving for constant action, and desire for useful sowings. In everything, let formality and routine be avoided. All, from the little to the great, are identically laborers, and they work not from fear but on account of conscience, or rather from joy. Surely, if one has not realized this joy, it means that one has not yet reflected on what enlightenment is in all domains, in all fields, in all possibilities.

I shall be glad to hear that you are flooded with correspondence as before, that you haven't enough time for everything that you would like to do. In this indomitable desire for creativeness will be your strength and youthfulness.

THE IMPERATIVE

[*The Scholar*. Palghat, Vol. XIV, No. 5,
February, 1939, pp. 233–236]

WHAT sort of work should claim our immediate attention? Everyday routine is, in itself, a very necessary form of work, and any conscientious labor has value; but there are so many complications in the world of today that we ought to, first of all, select the work that is of the utmost importance.

But how are we to know when a task is of the utmost importance and how to prevent it from being overlooked amid the hurry of our daily routine?

In these days of upheaval, such a matter is of the highest importance.

There is nothing unnecessary in everyday, routine work, or it would have been long ago excluded; nonetheless, we ought to give attention, at the same time, to the guiding principle of our times.

There is a saying often used in the navy, "do your best," by which every man is called upon to do his best in the way of knowledge, resourcefulness, and courage.

This will have a tendency to rouse every man to a feeling of obligation and responsibility.

A command such as "every man is expected to do his duty" is no longer personal but refers to the urgent circumstances with which every man has to deal with it to the best of his ability.

The worker has to decide if he will act at once or wait until later. Should he decide to wait, this will also be a form of action, since he is only holding up until certain invisible circumstances have coordinated.

Should he decide to act, however, then he ought to go carefully and adopt the best methods. Once he has begun the fight, he should beware of useless blows, for an inexperienced fighter can damage the most precious blade.

It is not always easy to decide what task is the most urgent. Experience, however, that gives us the faculty of intuition will gradually accustom us to taking rapid decisions.

Intuition is always immediate and direct, whereas calculation is often deceptive.

He who is guided by intuition can generally discriminate even in the most complicated situation. Amid much that seems urgent and new, there is a great deal that is obsolete and superfluous.

Whoever, despite the dangers and obstacles of the way, can discern the vital issues knows what is required.

He is not surprised to know that such imperative undertakings are surrounded by the utmost dangers and obstacles, because the powers of darkness are always present where life makes its appearance.

To select what is most urgent does not mean to choose what is easiest. Only worthless Maia surrounds the mirages of easy attainment. In fairy tales, we often hear of three paths, and the one that entails the least loss is the shortest. Where the risk is great, there the discovery is great, and, in fact, there lies the guarantee.

Perhaps you will think this is a matter for fairy tales, but even fairy tales warn us that there is a world of difference between words and deeds.

In historical narratives, we generally meet with little more than symbolical hieroglyphs of achievement—panther leaps, as it were.

But the panther has to collect his whole strength before leaping, and this itself is a form of activity.

Jackals accompany their movements with howling and screaming, which is according to their character. From animals, we can get a glimpse of what bloodthirstiness really is and come to see that coarseness and cruelty are out of place in the new world of the future.

All worthy activity is far removed from cruelty and bloodthirstiness and is rooted in steadfastness and in the effort to strive on to new ways of life.

Even wells will dry up, and time is needed for fresh moisture to gather. If the well has been bored in the right place, then the water will naturally replenish itself, provided you give it time.

But, as the saying is, "Do not spit in the well, this water is for drinking."

Many foolish travelers have allowed their wells to be contaminated, never expecting to return to them again. Often enough, however, circumstances have obliged them to do so.

The moment is, of course, one of great tension. What is most needed is probably near to hand but requires the concentration of all our attention if we are to discover it.

Nature is always calm before a storm, and an experienced traveler will never mistake this calm for a sign of fine weather.

I know that it is not easy to avoid being agitated when urgent events are knocking at the door, and amid the noise and turmoil of the present hour, there is the danger that we may overlook this inner rapping.

Inwardly, and to an even greater extent outwardly, all the different strata of life are seething, and what is most urgent and needful is being dispersed in effervescence, in sparks, and in splashes of light.

How are we to gauge what is best, what is most needful, and where is the measure of the great and small?

Everyone has read stories concerning people who failed to recognize what was good for them; it was only when it was too late that they began to recover their sight and tear their hair.

It is a common sight to see travelers arriving too late for the boat. The gangway has been lifted, and the unfortunate traveler is left behind, gesticulating amid the fluttering handkerchiefs of the crowd that has come to see their friends off.

Perhaps it was urgent for the traveler to leave with this particular boat and he had been detained by some chance circumstance. It is in such cases that we ought to remember the sayings, "Act according to your ability," "Act when it is necessary," "Act when it is urgent."

This threefold action—according to capacity, necessity, and urgency—denotes what is essential. In such noble intensity, there is the secret of what is inevitable, urgent, and imperative. The younger the heart, the quicker it responds to what is imperative.

A youthful heart, however, is not to be measured in years, for many frozen and senile hearts are found among the newborn. Many hearts are so darkened by coarseness and cruelty that their hardheartedness will show itself in their daily conduct of affairs.

Even good people are sometimes hardhearted, but this prevents them from realizing what is essential. One-sided measures will prevent one from approaching the necessary, and even after collecting all accumulations, we shall still sense a certain deficiency.

To recognize the imperative supposes a certain comprehensiveness, and requires that sense of synthesis that is the true sign of culture.

The task of culture will always be to outline the principal traits of what is most needful. This is just. But among the problems of culture, some will require years of preparation, others immediate action. And we must know which of these requires immediate fulfillment.

Think, think, think; necessity demands intensity of thought. Only in such intense energy will the radiant fire disclose what is imperative.

Yet the outline of this severe and beautiful face does not terrify; on the contrary, it attracts the heart and arms it with new strength.

"And as the vague lines of a secret letter suddenly stand out above the flame, so will a vision appear before you all at once."

A FRIEND OF MANKIND

[*Flamma: A Quarterly.* Liberty, No. 6, Summer, 1939, pp. 75–76]

A GREAT friend of mankind has passed away. I speak of Charles Crane. Manifold and fruitful was his life, and in all parts of the world, he will be warmly remembered. Crane belonged to one of the old American families, and his life was one of ceaseless activity. In childhood, being drawn to the East, he joined a schooner as a shipboy, and this first cruise of his showed all his longing for far-off lands.

Charles's father was one of the largest industrialists in America and wished his son to stay in the factory. From his fifteenth year, Charles was acquainted with the workshop, and this gave him a practical knowledge of the industry. Later, we see him in close partnership with Westinghouse, but such an activity never filled his soul. Gradually, he turned away from direct participation in the factories and dedicated himself to the wider activities of the diplomat and humanist.

We remember Charles Crane as ambassador in Peking, where he is highly esteemed, and, afterward, as an honorary advisor to the Chinese Government. We know of Crane's friendship and meetings with Ibn Saud of Arabia, with Feisal of Iraq, and with the leaders of Egypt. After this, he goes to India and then to Russia. If his activity was great, the significance of his humanitarian work was greater, as a multitude of facts can witness.

Who sent a shipload of provisions to Mt. Athos to

save the monastery from starvation and poverty?—Crane. Who helped Czechoslovakia and Masaryk?—Crane. Who gave funds for educating students in other countries?—Crane. In Syria, in Switzerland, and in China, students and scholars will always remember the generous hand that helped them on their difficult way. In his hospitable home, one could always meet with scholars, writers, artists, diplomats, and social workers—in other words, outstanding people from various countries. For some, he arranged lecture tours—for others, recitals, stage work, and exhibitions. He helped universities, museums, and hospitals. Vast anonymous support was given everywhere where there was a need for it. Verily, one can say that no one ever left Crane without some encouragement and heartfelt assistance. A special trait of Crane's character was his extreme sensitiveness and responsiveness. No one could stop him when he felt that he could help. Many cultural and philanthropic organizations had his name on their lists of honor. He was also an Honorary Advisor of our institutions.

More than once during his travels, Crane was subject to great dangers, but nothing could keep him back. In Iraq, he escaped death from a shot fired by bandits thanks to a happy coincidence. His best humanitarian deeds were sometimes misinterpreted. Crane's attachment to the East was remarkable, and not only did he like to travel in the East, but he had a deep understanding of its people and its majestic beauty. He did not cross Asia or Egypt as a casual tourist but as an old friend.

To us Russians, the name of Crane is especially dear. He was often in Russia, knew and appreciated the Russian people, and admired Russia's ancient art. The last time he was in Moscow, about two years ago, we received a remarkable letter in which he gave favorable impressions of his trip. The opinion of such a connoisseur is most valuable. If only the Russian people could have more such friends!

Crane's art collection was comprised of Russian and Oriental art. He had many Russian paintings, tapestries, and other art objects. On the walls of his houses and villas, one could see Samarkand, Mt. Athos, Rostov the Great, Benares, Tibet, and the Himalaya—in other words, everything to which his great soul was attracted. Toward the end of his life, after a severe illness, he expressed his desire to see the Near East. And last September, he visited Egypt and, for the last time, admired the grandeur of the pyramids.

Before his passing, Crane wrote to us for my painting *And We Open the Gates.* His spirit was already aspiring to the open gates, where dwells eternal beauty and where thought creates the future happy life. On February 14th, Charles Crane left this earthly world, but his memory will live on in all countries. His many friends will cherish in their hearts the memory of this great friend of mankind.

CONSTANT CARE

[*The Scholar.* Palghat, Vol. XIV, No. 9, June, 1939, pp. 403–405]

OUR committees are already enquiring about what their situation is likely to be after the Pact. They realize that official ratification may mean that the Pact Societies will be excluded from taking any initiative or from cooperating with their different governments.

The opposite, however, is likely to occur. The more we progress in this matter of safeguarding cultural treasures, the more we are likely to require the cooperation of public and private enterprises.

Culture can never be the work of a single government; rather is it the expression of a whole nation—of all nations.

Cooperation between all nations is indispensable if we are to make any advance in the matter.

Educational institutions, and all those other societies that exist for progress and enlightenment, must necessarily cooperate with all the elements in the nation.

The closer the connection is between our museum societies, the more active our committees are likely to be with the schools, and cooperation more lively in every sense.

The same will occur with the application of the Pact for the Preservation of Cultural Treasures. Quite apart from the activity of government committees and institutions, we cannot dispense with private assistance or the initiative of well-wishers.

The committee that participated in the work of the

Pact negotiations will remain the best collaborator in the future. If our committees have shown their activity in multifarious directions, then they are all the better equipped for cooperating with government activities.

Remember how many useful initiatives have been taken in the last four years, and that in addition to three international conferences, lectures have been arranged in many countries.

Many times, attention has been drawn to the Pact in schools, many articles have appeared in the press, and processions in which the banner has appeared have been organized so as to give an idea of cultural values.

Besides the local committees, the Washington Convention established a Pact Committee that gave a permanent character to the Pact and made it the custodian of those resolutions that were drawn up at the Washington Convention to defend and preserve all cultural values.

It is most probable that this permanent committee will grow in importance and attract more and more attention, together with an increasing number of collaborators from the arts and sciences.

So wide is the scope of work that all newcomers will be welcomed with joy and friendship, for we require the cooperation of all sections of the community.

The need for safeguarding cultural values ought to be realized by every class of society. It should be taught in schools and colleges, and teachers should do their best to enlighten everyone as to its urgent character.

Several of our committees have no doubt realized that a large section of the community is, as it were, shut out from taking any part, or interest, in cultural activities. They have had to fight their way to get a hearing for the simplest propositions and have often encountered opposition even in intellectual circles.

In short, they have no illusions, knowing that there will always be difficulties.

The way of culture is the way of the cross and one that is never likely to be an easy one. There are many, however, who are ready to raise their voices but will do little to save the situation.

There will be meetings held on behalf of culture in which much will be said but little achieved, but this should not deter us in our determination to raise aloft the Banner of Culture.

The work of all these groups, societies, committees, and collaborators will always be one of great variety, and the work is likely to grow in all directions since it depends upon the world structure of life itself.

Governments ought to be glad of the work of volunteers, who so willingly give their time to help in matters that, after all, are of the highest concern to the state.

The Committee itself is a center of friendly cooperation, able to attract the goodwill of everyone. It is unlimited in the number of its members and can be separated into subdivisions, sections, commissions, and made to conform with anything that will promote the good work.

Let constancy be expressed by a desire for action, cooperation, benevolence, and altruism. Where the word Culture is pronounced, there let altruism grow so that the work of enlightenment can proceed with joy and mutual confidence.

Every friend acquired is a pathway to culture; every enemy overthrown is a victory for light. The salvation of beauty and knowledge is itself a lofty form of prayer.

JOY

[*The Educational Review.* Madras, Vol. XLV, No. 3,
March, 1939, pp. 145–146]

MUSIC was one of our earliest delights. We can still remember the piano tuner who used to come to the house—a little old man, completely blind and led by his granddaughter. After he had tuned the piano, he always played something. The piano was a Bluthner, quite a good instrument, with the mark, *Leschitizky.* The blind man was an excellent pianist, and I never forget his playing. We used to wait impatiently until the tuning was over, fearing that someone might interrupt the playing. The drawing room was in blue, and on the wall was a picture of our beloved *Kanchenjunga* with a roseate background. The blind man played to perfection. It is strange how well the blind can play!

Later, at the Bolshoi Theatre, we saw *Ruslan and Ludmila, A Life for the Tsar,* and then followed the ballets *Roiana, The Bayadére, The Pharaoh's Daughter,* and *Le Corsair.* The orchestra seemed to play magic notes of gold. The conductor was coming with his wand, and we were anxious that everyone be seated. "The gentleman with the stick has taken his place," I whispered, to prevent latecomers spoiling the magical first notes by their entrance. On the curtain near us was the image of a faun pursuing amorini. It was unpleasant to sit in a box by the side of the faun, and we preferred the middle seats.

The Italian opera pleased us less; Mazzini and Patti did not impress us. *Rigoletto, Traviata,* and *Lucia* were foreign to our taste. *Aida* and *L'Africana* were nearer to us, and the chorus of Africans singing of Brahma and Vishnu became one of our piano selections. We were not allowed, however, to play in the daytime near father's study.

Later, new vistas were opened up with the Belayev concerts and the *Snow Maiden* of Rimsky-Korsakov. The name of Mussorgsky, uncle to Elena Ivanovna, came to us from afar.

We were among the first to subscribe to the Wagnerian cycle. It is curious today to think that cultured people of that time considered Wagner a cacophonist.

Probably all great achievements have to go through the furnace of mockery and denial.

There was more joy in childhood. If the world is at present devoid of joy, if the world is at present drowned in ugly hatred, then one wants the more to remember the true joy that creates enthusiasm. From the first school days, I remember Mark Twain's beautiful *The Prince and the Pauper*. It is remarkable how Mark Twain's name victoriously went all over Russia. The writer found an approach to the human soul, and convincingly and simply he called to eternal truths. Many of our generation will remember this great name with gratitude.

In the same spirit, I remember Zola, who through his novel dedicated to Manet and Manet's fight for art, opened to me the gateways to the Beauty of the battle of life. There were many such precious way-signs. And after many, many years, one wishes to send to these authors one's heartiest thoughts. In the turmoil of life, much is lost, and it is remarkable to witness what selection life is making itself. When we look back, we see, as if from a hill, the whole road of the past and the runes on the rock. It is said that childhood becomes especially clear with years, but this is not quite true.

We only look more piercingly and seek for those beneficial milestones that helped to build the subsequent
path.

And to these good way-signs, we dedicate our first
joy, our first imagination, and our first gratitude.

SOWING

[*The Scholar.* Palghat, Vol. XIV, No. 10, July, 1939, p. 449]

CAN anyone foresee which sapling will thrive best in the forest and which will be the first to perish? And so, with sowing, who can say which will prove to be the best field when so many factors have to be taken into consideration?

The most experienced gardener cannot always say which tree will produce the finest blossom. A good sower will not complain because he does not always see the result of his work. And so, in matters of culture, it is impossible to say when the sturdiest shoots will appear. Nor can we predict to what extent alteration or dissolution can engender fresh offshoots. I remember that A. A. Golenishchev-Kutuzov told us that he did not desire to see his collection housed in a museum. "Let it be dispersed, provided it gives new collectors the same pleasure as it gave to me."

He was not only a lover of art, who spoke in this way, but a poet. He knew the joys of collecting and loved to be creative. He knew that such joy is particularly vivid when it concerns private collections rather than museums. For them, it is a matter of real admiration and creative faculty. Like a poet, he felt that every creation has its own destiny. Some are destined to take root in one spot for a long time, others to go touring the world like travelers, giving joy in unexpected places.

We cannot say which joy is the greater, nor can we predict where a work of art will have its greatest influence. It may be that the youthful heart will derive its highest inspiration from home, where the routine of life is often lit up with the beauty of real art. Everyone knows how frequently failure has engendered an effort to greater things. It has been said, "There is no fortune to which misfortune has not contributed." We have seen in what unexpected ways fresh creatures can arise. All is in movement. This constant movement that transcends human reason, gives rise to new tensions that sharpen our forces and bring about a spirit of creativeness. People do not know what wanderings are in store for them, nor can they foresee the roads of the future. Let everything go forward toward a new conception.

WORK IN COMMON

[*The Scholar*. Palghat, Vol. XIV, No. 10, July, 1939, p. 450]

WHILE an exhibition of my paintings was being held at the Kansas City Museum, a certain Mrs. Holmes had the charming idea of presenting my picture *Lord of the Night* to the museum, in the name of the children. The plan was adopted, and the children responded since children always like to be given the more serious work of adults.

Appeals were made through the papers, children's parades held, and, on the whole, the scheme proved successful.

It is always a great joy for me to see youth participating in such movements, especially when, as in this instance, they were not forced to do so.

On the contrary, once the idea had been given, children of all ages responded to it spontaneously. There are quite a number of such cooperative movements going on in the world, and the more the better, for we cannot sufficiently attract youth to the idea of working toward a common construction. And, in the last resort, for whom is everything being built? For future generations, for youth itself. If youth be taught to cooperate all over the world, this will make a link with the future. Much has been said about the differences and the misunderstandings that separate the members of different generations.

Senility, however, does not depend upon the generation one belongs to, since there are aged people who are young in spirit and youngsters who are often quite senile.

The question is not one of age but of the thinking processes. The more a person is attracted to work in common from his early years, the more will he be accustomed to think of the common welfare and to retain a spirit of youth.

Today, there are widespread movements in which whole populations show a tendency to collaborate in the direction of public work, and people should not only be admitted to such tasks but should be made to feel that they are collaborators. This sense of collaboration and responsibility will tend to engender a healthy strain of thought and enable people to discover and rejoice in all that is beautiful.

Encourage cooperation.

LOSSES

[*The Twentieth Century.* Allahabad, Vol. V,
September, 1939, pp. 942–943]

IN the latest editions of the old masters, there are given, in the backs of the books, lists of their works that have disappeared. Some of them are known from engravings, others were copied while still extant, but the originals themselves have apparently vanished without a trace. This could have happened in the many fires and during various periods of vandalism and religious persecution, such as in the time of Savonarola. In fact, there are still being discovered on occasion, such *lost* objects in the most unexpected circumstances. It may be recalled that not long ago an excellent Vermeer was discovered, and an unquestionable Rembrandt was bought at auction in Brussels for one hundred francs. Apart from destructions, old pictures have frequently been painted over from completely incomprehensible motives. This happened with a picture of Dürer and with many outstanding Italian and Netherlands artists. I myself once bought a very good Van der Weyden that had been entirely painted over. Our times should provide still greater surprises, not only with old pictures but also with our own. We know about the loss of *Unkrada, Battle at Kerzhenets, Kazan, Summons, Campaign,* and many other pictures. It was told that during the war in one Polish castle, there were destroyed a great number of paintings, among them, six of mine. At the same time, there was found one of my pictures on the isolated island of Saaremaa. In Switzerland, there turned up a sketch for *Idols*, which had been believed lost a long time ago. Verily, the ways of art are inscrutable. It will be remembered how in 1906, in America, there were sold eight hundred Russian pictures at a forced sale to satisfy the debts of the Commissioner of the exhibit, Gruenwald. Among them were works of Repin, the brothers Makovsky, Musatov, and many other well-known artists. Up until now, it has remained completely unknown to where was dispersed all this quantity of works. Of my own, there were in this number, seventy-five studies of Russian antiquity and the paintings *Meeting of the Elders* and *Pakov*. Some of them were sold to a museum in California, but twenty-five items disappeared without any trace. It has been said that they are somewhere in Canada. At one of the casual auctions in London, I chanced to see two pictures of Vereshchagin. It was asked where to look for his entire Indian series? Inscrutable is the fate of art. Eternal are the wanderers.

March 1939.

MANY EXAMPLES

[*The Twentieth Century.* Allahabad, Vol. V,
September, 1939, pp. 943–944]

Anatole Erance writes thus:

"Numerous instances could be given; I shall mention only one. Some fifteen years ago in a volunteers' examination, the Military Board gave the candidates, as a piece of dictation, an unsigned excerpt that was quoted in many periodicals and made much fun of, rousing the ridicule of very cultivated readers. "Where," they asked, "did these military fellows dig up such ludicrous phrases?" Yet, as a matter of fact, they had taken them from a very noble book. This was Michelet and Michelet at his best.

"The wag who laughed loudest was an enthusiastic admirer of Michelet. The passage is an admirable piece of writing, yet to arouse the most admiration, it had to bear the author's name. It is exactly thus with any page written by the hand of man. And, on the contrary, a great name excites extravagant praise. Victor Cousin discovered sublimities in Pascal that have since been recognized as a copyist's errors. For example, he went into ecstasies over *raccourcis d'abime,* which is solely the result of erroneous reading. It is difficult to imagine M. Victor Cousin admiring the same expression in the pages of a contemporary. The rhapsodies of a certain Vrain-Lucas were favorably received by the Academy of Sciences under the august names of Pascal and Descartes. Ossian seemed the equal of Homer as long as people thought him an ancient bard. He has been neglected since it was learned he originated with Macpherson."

In truth, there are many examples of unfairness. It has happened that a Rembrandt was thrown out of an exhibition, and a Corot was not allowed to enter. In 1904, I proposed setting up an anonymous exhibition so as to provide an occasion to deliberate about quality. But this idea seemed terrible! Anything might happen. Unknowns might be exalted, while those who had been honored might lose their regalia. No doubt Anatole France many times experienced the conventionality of opinions and well knew all the changes of the tide. Antiquary Smirnov said: "What of the signature? A signature is a matter of thirty *kopecks*." Thus do things come and go. To one it will be advantageous to belittle, to another it will seem useful to exalt. But for all that, "Beauty will save the world."

April 1939.

GLORY OF HELLAS

[*The Twentieth Century*. Allahabad, Vol. V,
September, 1939, pp. 944-946]

L ONDON newspapers reported on May 8th the discovery of remarkable finds at Delphi. It is said that the treasures that have been found are regarded by French and Greek archaeologists as not only the most valuable ever found in Greece but probably in the whole world. The finds were made by scientists who, on removing some slabs on the sacred road that leads to the Temple of Apollo, discovered a large cellar containing statues of pure gold and ivory, made in the sixth century BC. The sculptural treasures had been placed in a well hidden under the sacred road. The upper layer, under which the treasures were found, was of ashes, which proves that the sculptures were placed there at the time of a great fire. Golden garments for statues were discovered, also many golden *fibuli*, earrings, and plaques with beautifully chiseled animal figures. Continuing excavations in a northerly direction, the archaeologists found another well also filled with bronze and gold objects. The French archaeologist Pierre de La Coste-Messelièr states that all treasures found in the wells show definite traces of oriental influence and were probably produced in the Greek colonies in Asia Minor.

There are three remarkable circumstances connected with these discoveries. First, near the ancient and magnificent Temple of Apollo, one might expect to discover beautiful finds; and this has now been done. Second, there exists a prophecy that at Delphi, at some important date, significant treasures would be found; and they have been found now. And third, the statement of the French archaeologist about Eastern influence is most indicative.

In a large part of India, Hellenic influences have been discovered. And now we hear the authoritative news that these new archaeological finds in such a central place as Delphi show Eastern influence. At the same time, we should remember that these finds refer to the best period of Hellenic art. Now, if we coordinate the Hellenic influence in the East and the Eastern influence in Greece at its best period, we come to a most interesting conclusion. The great Orient was the cradle of Hellenic art, which is equally great, and which laid the foundation for the future apotheosis of art.

"This is for the future," said Sophocles. The same could be said of Hellenic art and philosophy in general. It is very remarkable to observe what elements for the future were embodied in the Hellenic creations of Phidias, Praxiteles, Lysippus, Apelles, and in those of the mighty phalanx of artists of all domains. Besides the living contact of this art with philosophy, or rather with philosophers, both art and philosophy were themselves vital. Pythagoras, Plato, Anaxagoras, Socrates, and all the remarkable thinkers before whom the entire world bowed, were themselves, in the deepest sense, artists. And was not Pericles, the great leader of his people, a true patron of Beauty and Thought? And what other nation had nine muses, the guardians of all branches of art and knowledge? It is most significant that in all ages and countries the Hellenic art was always esteemed as the highest expression of human genius. And we know that the greatest thinkers of Hellas were in constant touch with Egypt, India, and all the cradles of wisdom. This relationship was by no means due to imitation; it arose from a kindred affinity of the Great and Beautiful. We see the brilliant epoch of Gandhara; we know what deep traces Hellas left in Scythian art. Let us remember the Hellenic influence in Egypt, in Asia Minor, and throughout Asia. Truly, by its inexhaustible, convincing vitality, Hellenic Art found reverence and followers everywhere. In academies, it was a custom, until recently, to copy Hellenic classical sculptures and then to go over to life studies. But I have myself always advised the reverse order, and let Hellenic studies follow after life classes because only an experienced mind can appreciate the real splendor of the Hellenic art heritage.

I am writing these lines in the Himalayas, high above the river Beas, which winds its way below like a silver ribbon. On this very river, Alexander the Great halted in his eastward march. Thus, even here in the Himalayas, Hellenic memories are awakened. The whole of South Russia is also filled with unfading Hellenic masterpieces. Wherever Hellenic colonies were founded, there art flourishes. It is surely the gift of the Gods that wherever there are Hellenic traces, there is also a record of Beauty. True greatness is there, where life and art are inseparable. And this union leads to immortality!

June 1939.

CORMON

[*The Twentieth Century.* Allahabad, Vol. VI, October, 1939, p. 14]

IN the academy that Fernand Cormon directed in Paris, many excellent things were taught to us. Some considered him to be a dry, formal type of teacher and too academic. I must say that I never found this to be so myself. Speaking of his own work, Cormon said— "If I had to begin again, I would be a sculptor."

One has only to study his *Cain* in the Luxembourg Gallery to see the truth of this remark. He was not a colorist, and yet he showed himself a very able teacher in the use of color. Looking at my own sketches, he once remarked, "We are too refined, we shall learn from you." When I told him that I preferred to work alone and did not care much for studio work, he answered sympathetically: "Yes, one can only become an artist if one be left alone; nearly all schools are useless. If you can afford it, rent a studio and work alone; I shall always be ready to supervise your work."

This does not seem to show that he was of the dry and academic type. It recalls Sargent's saying after meeting with certain members of the Royal Academy—"They were far more human than I had expected."

His pupils were aware that there were two Cormons. The first would enter the Academy and begin to correct the drawings without further discussion; the second would invite certain students to his house, and on holidays one could find animated groups gathered around quite another Cormon. On these occasions, he reminded me of Anatole France, for his talk overflowed with clever and brilliant remarks. He knew how to praise and, at the same time, give valuable advice. All sorts of work were brought to him, from studies and rough sketches to finished works. He liked my *Idols, March of Vladimir to Korsun, Portage, Ravens,* and the sketches made for *The Elders Gather.* One might have expected that he would have been shocked by the color scheme of *Idols,* but he only exclaimed, "farouche, farouche" and, showing it to the other students, remarked, "This might well be for the future." For me, his praise, "You have style" was inspiring forever.

A NARROW ESCAPE

[*The Twentieth Century.* Allahabad, Vol. VI, October, 1939, p. 19]

IN the early spring of 1907, I left with Elena Ivanovna[*] for Finland to find a place in which to spend summer. We started off on a cold day wearing fur coats, but in Viborg, it became warmer, although people were still going about in sleighs. We engaged the services of a Finn, who had a small roan horse, and who was somewhat morose, and started off with him to an address somewhere outside of the town. After passing Viborg castle, we descended to a sort of snow-covered plain where there were thawed patches, and we went swiftly forward. To our astonishment, the patches rapidly increased in size and water began to make its appearance. After going on for some time, we realized that we were crossing a large lake on loose ice. The distant shores appeared as a narrow strip of land, and we found ourselves surrounded on all sides by open water. The only way out that remained to us was the way we had come. Our driver was panic-stricken and beat his horse, which now sensed the danger and ran with all its strength. At times it broke through the ice and was up to its knees, but the driver succeeded in dragging it up with the reins. We called to him to turn back, but he only cracked his whip in reply, saying that it was impossible to leave the ribbon-like road. Water now began to enter the sleigh, and things did look rather grave. Elena Ivanovna kept on repeating:

---

[*]   Madame Helena Roerich.

"What a stupid way to perish!" The situation was more or less hopeless, and once the ribbon of thin ice gave in, we should all be precipitated into the depths of the lake. The horse now galloped furiously, and there was no use to use the whip. The shore began to approach, and we could see people running along and waving in despair. We soon realized that this was because of our situation, but the horse continued to put on top speed. When we drove in on the sloping granite shore, we saw that the ice was breaking up into sections. The little horse had run in a miraculous way with the sledge plunging through the water, and now the people gathered around and led him in. They found fault with the driver, saying that he knew perfectly well that the lake had been closed to traffic for at least three days, and one of the coast guards took his name, while all were astonished at our narrow escape and our calmness. We had relied on the speed of this little Finnish horse, and he had seen us through. Among the many dangers we have gone through, this of Finland was not the least.

COLLECTORSHIP

[*The Twentieth Century.* Allahabad, Vol. VI, October, 1939, p. 20]

WE were often asked why we collected pictures, especially those of the Netherlands' school. Yet who has never dreamed of Van Eyck, Memling, Van der Weyden, Van Reymerswaele, David, Matsys? And then, there is always an element of chance in collecting. Some things come easier than others, and one direction proves easier than another.

I myself have gotten much pleasure from the works of Bles, Bruegel, Patinir, Lucas van Leyden, and Cranach. After these, I became fascinated by the decorative qualities and construction in the work of Savery, Bril, Momper, Elsheimer, Lombard, Avercamp, Goltzius, Van der Velde the elder, and Coninck. After which I naturally took to Rubens, Van Goyen, Van Ostade, Van der Neer, Lievens, Neefs, Teniers, and Ruysdael, and no one was surprised that these great masters should enter my collection. But the primitives with their vibrant color and wealth of composition fascinated me more than all. Elena Ivanovna was so taken by the primitives that the most attractive masterpieces of the seventeenth century failed to draw her attention.

The discovery of such pictures was itself a memorable period of my life. Many curious things took place. A Rubens was once discovered in an old bookbinding. On another occasion, we discovered a Van Orley that had been worked over with an unintelligible design, on the top of which was the image of a hideous, old man.

E.I. liked to clean the pictures herself, and nothing delighted her more than to discover beneath the coating of paint, a head by some authentic master. In this way, she came across Savery's *Noah's Ark,* on which had been painted some dark composition.

We failed to restore a Lucas van Leyden on which a landscape had been painted. Another version of this picture appears in the Louvre.

A Peter Bruegel was discovered by chance. At a sale, I had been asked to buy something. There were many modern pictures that had no interest for us, and the saleswoman was disappointed. At last, I remarked on a small, dark red picture up over a mirror, between two windows. The seller said it was not worth getting down and that it did not matter if I bought nothing at all. I insisted, and she said: "Well, if I go to the trouble of getting it down, you will have to buy it, and place twenty-five rupees on the table in guarantee." When we took it home, this little copper plate was so dark that we could not make out the subject. Later, when we began to clean it and clear away the coatings of grime, a winter scene by Bruegel appeared. In the same way, we discovered the *Guitarist* of Van Dyck. A considerable price had been fixed, but E. I., without waiting for us to come to terms, began cleaning it. You can imagine our consternation when the owner came for a settlement. Fortunately, nothing was lost, and a Bloemaert, which had been painted over with angels, came to light.

We had many adventures of this type. The old Netherlanders gave us much joy, and so did the Primitives, which are so near to the modern school.

ASIA

[*The Twentieth Century.* Allahabad, Vol. VI, October, 1939, p. 23]

THE East is quite a relative conception and not a matter of geography. If you go South from Paris until you reach Algiers, you will find yourself in the East. But should you go eastward from Algiers until you reach Greece or Romania, then you will find yourself back again in the West. Moreover, the boundaries of Asia are indefinite. This was noted long ago and brought into use such terms as Australasia and Eurasia. No one could say why Astrakhan, the Caucasus, or the Crimea should not be considered Asia. The limit of the Ural Mountains—the conventional borderline between Asia and Europe—only leads to confusion. Once upon a time, ignorant and foolish people considered it below their dignity to be called Asiatics, but later, through the efforts of a few enlightened people, such absurd prejudices were dropped. A clear-sighted poet once said, "Certainly we are Asiatics"—and why not? Is not Siberia, the Russian treasure-house, itself a part of Asia?

From my very earliest years, I was drawn to the heart of Asia. The names of Przhevalsky and Potanin had long attracted me. The Mongol epos and the treasures of India had always dazzled my imagination. From the earliest times, the Slav has always listened attentively to the fables of the East. Relations with the Orient were much closer than Western historians have related. Without speaking of the Oriental character of Byzance, of the treasure of the Russian East, one can note how the pictorial arts of Europe have retained Asiatic influences. The heart of Asia is the heart of the world because all teachings and all wisdom come from there. Are not the North American Indians of Asiatic origin?

Our family was always destined to be connected with Asia. Friends were constantly arriving who had served in Asia or had information about it. We had professors of the Eastern faculty and from Siberia, professors from Tomsk. All these had much to say of the heart of Asia, and they advised me to lose no time in leaving for the vast expanses of the Orient. From my earliest years, recollections of Asia are connected with all the spiritual influences that have affected my life.

INDIA

[*The Twentieth Century.* Allahabad, Vol. VI, October, 1939, p. 24]

FROM early childhood, I seem to have had a connection with India. The name of our estate, Iswara, was recognized by Tagore as a Sanskrit word. In the reign of Catherine II, there lived in our neighborhood an Indian Rajah, and until quite recently, there were traces of a Mogul Park. We had an old picture in the house of a great snow-covered mountain. Afterward, I learned from Brian Hodgson's book that this was the celebrated Kanchenjunga.

An uncle of Elena Ivanovna went to India about the middle of the last century and subsequently appeared at a court ball in St. Petersburg in a beautiful Rajput costume. He again returned to India, and nothing more was heard of him. As far back as 1905, many pictures and sketches of mine were devoted to India. *Devasari, Lakshmi, The Way to India, The Boundary of the Kingdom, Krishna, Sons of India:* all of these, as well as *Desert Cities,* were painted long before I went to India.

From 1923 we have been in India, and since that time, our knowledge of the country, our love for it, and our many friends have continued to grow. In 1920, Rabindranath Tagore visited us in London and called us to India. After this, there appeared in Calcutta a long article in *The Modern Review* on my art, which was an introduction to India. Elena Ivanovna had for long known and loved the books of Ramakrishna and Vivekananda.

In the same year, we made a tour of the principal places of interest in India, beginning with Elephanta, Agra, Fatehpur Sikri, Benares, Sarnath. We visited the Ashrams of Ramakrishna, Adyar, Madurai, Ceylon, and everywhere we met with a cordial welcome. Connections were established, not only with the family of Tagore but with many representatives of philosophic thought—Swami Ramdas, Sri Vaswani, Swami Omkar, Swami Jagadiswarananda, Sri Swami Sadanand Sarasvati. Subsequently, we made friends with Jagadis Bose; corresponded with Anagarika Dharmapala, Ramananda Chatterjee, K. Iswara Dutt, Suniti Kumar Chatterji, and C. V. Raman. We established cordial relations with the artists Asit Kumar Haldar, Abanindranath and Gaganendranath Tagore, Bireswar Sen, Mukul Dey, Raval, and with the critics Gangoly, Mehta, Basu, Tandan, Bhattacharya, Chaturvedi, Cunchithapatham, Tampy, and Siriwardhana.

The Bose Institute, the Royal Asiatic Society of Bengal, Maha Bodhi, Nagari Pracharini Sabha, and the Indian Society of Oriental Arts elected me an honorary or life member.

At the instigation of Rai Krishnadasa, a separate hall was arranged for my work in the Bharata Kala Bhawan, and through the initiative of Rai Bahadur and Brij Mohan Vyas, the Municipal Museum in Allahabad also devoted a separate hall. Through the collaboration of Dr. J. H. Cousins, the Travancore Government acquired a whole group of my pictures for their State Gallery, Sri Chitralayam. So did Hyderabad. Other Indian States proposed to hold exhibitions.

From different quarters in India, we have received touching messages from many local organizations, such as the Congress of the Mahasabha, the Delhi Students Federation, Boy Scouts, Maha Bodhi, Stri Dharma, and The School of Peace.

Prefaces for books by Fatulla Khan, Teija Singh, Mohanlal, Kashyap, Bhanu Singh, Gupta, and others were given.

I shall not forget the "Builder of Modern Karachi," Jamshed Nusserwanji.

India received our Institute with kind hospitality. A hearty greeting to India.

NAGGAR

[*The Twentieth Century.* Allahabad, Vol. VI, October, 1939, p. 25]

WE came from Darjeeling and reached Kulu Valley—the ancient Kuluta. The banks of the Beas river are associated with the Rishi Vyasa, who compiled the Mahabharata, and with Alexander the Great, whose army passed close to here.

Through here went also Buddha and *Padma Sambhava*, and here lived Arjuna and other Pandavas. Not far distant is Manali—derived from *Manu.* Then there are the hot springs of Basistha and the valley of Manikaran Parvati with its silver ore. On the other side of the Rohtang Pass, there is already Tibetan scenery.

Here we found an abundance of all we needed. . . . Ancient Kuluta!

It was at Christmas in 1928 that we came to Naggar. We had not crossed the Beas River when we saw a house high up on the hill. "That is where we shall live," we exclaimed; but we were told that the house, which was on the Rajah of Mandi's estate, was not to be had, and that our wishes were out of the question. If a thing is destined, however, it has to be done, and so, despite the many obstacles, we had our way.

To the North of us—Manali, Arjun Gufa, Jagatsukh, Basistha, and beyond, the snowy Rohtang. Here is the ancient road to Tibet, Kailas, Ladakh, Khotan, the Gobi, and Altai. To the East—the Chanderkhani Pass and beyond, Malana, Spiti, Tibet. To the West— Bara Bhangal and beyond, the mountains of Kashmir,

Pir Panjal, and the Pamirs. To the South—the road to Shimla, Mandi, and Lake Ravalsar, and beyond, the torrid plains of India.

Naggar is a very ancient place. There are several very old temples and, according to Chinese travelers, at one time there were Buddhist viharas, of which no trace remains. There is a tradition that during the iconoclastic rule of Langdarma in Tibet, the sacred books were hidden here. Narsingh, the protector of the valley, sometimes appears as an old man clad in white, and Guga Chohan, an ancient Rajput Raja, is revered as another guardian of the valley.

The valley contains three hundred and sixty gods. We have a stipulation in writing between the god *Jamlu*, the British Government, and ourselves as to the use of the water. Trumpets sound and the drums thunder when the gods visit each other on festive occasions. In the forest is a temple where the anchorite Pahari Baba dwelled.

Pines, deodars, and oaks still clothe the slopes, although many woods have been felled. From the ancient road at the foot of the hill, one can hear the caravan bells. There is magic in the sound of the caravan bell—Whence? Whither? What news?

THE ROERICH PACT
THE BANNER OF PEACE

[*Flamma: A Quarterly.* Liberty, No. 7, Autumn, 1939, pp. 16–62]

THIS sign of the triad, which is to be found all over the world, may have several meanings. Some interpret it as a symbol of the past, present, and future enclosed in the ring of eternity. Others consider that it refers to religion, science, and art held together in the circle of culture. But whatever the interpretation, the sign itself is of the most universal character.

The oldest of Indian symbols, Chintamani, the sign of happiness, is composed of this symbol, and one can find it in the Temple of Heaven in Peking. It appears in the Three Treasures of Tibet, on the breast of the Christ in Memling's well-known painting, on the Madonna of Strasbourg; on the shields of the Crusaders, and the coat of arms of the Templars. It can be seen on the blades of the famous Caucasian swords known as Gurda.

It appears as a symbol in a number of philosophical systems; it can be found on the images of Gessar Khan and Rigden Djapo; on the *Tamga* of Timurlane, and on the coat of arms of the Popes. It is to be seen in the works of ancient Spanish painters and of Titian, and on the ancient ikons of St. Nicholas in Bari and that of St. Sergius and the Holy Trinity.

It can be found on the coat of arms of the city of Samarkand, on Ethiopian and Coptic antiquities, on the rocks of Mongolia, on Tibetan rings, on the breast ornaments of Lahul, Ladakh, and all the Himalayan countries, and on the pottery of the Neolithic Age.

It is conspicuous on Buddhist banners. The same sign is branded on Mongolian steeds. Nothing, then, could be more appropriate for assembling all the races than this symbol, which is no mere ornament but a sign that carries with it a deep meaning.

It has existed for immense periods of time and is to be found throughout the world. No one, therefore, can pretend that it belongs to any particular sect, confession, or tradition, and it represents the evolution of consciousness in all its varied phases.

When it is a question of defending the world's treasures, no better symbol could be selected, for it is universal, of immense antiquity, and carries with it a meaning that should find an echo in every heart.

Today, when humanity is burying its treasures to save them from destruction, the Banner of Peace stands for other principles. It affirms that works of art and of genius are universal and above national distinctions; it proclaims, "*Noli me tangere.* Do not treat the world's treasures in a sacrilegious way."

TO ALL DEFENDERS OF
CULTURAL TREASURES

[*The Maha-Bodhi.* Calcutta, Vol. XLVII, No. 10,
1939, pp. 468–469]

THE thunder of the European war again demands that active attention should be paid to the defense of cultural treasures. A pact to this effect is under consideration by many of the European governments and has already been signed by twenty-one governments of the Americas. No doubt, since military operations have already begun, it is hardly to be expected that any agreement could take place during actual warfare. Yet the activities of our committees should at all times be fruitful. Remembering the position in which the protection of cultural treasures was at the beginning of 1914, we must say that, at present, this important question has definitely been given much more attention by governments and public institutions. Doubtless the activities of our committees have had beneficial influence upon public opinion and have contributed to such an increase of attention. Besides government decrees, public opinion is the first defender of national treasures that have a universal value. During the last great war, we applied our utmost efforts to draw attention to the fact that it is criminal to destroy historical, scientific, and artistic monuments. Then during recent conflagrations, as, for instance, in Spain and China, we happened to hear that our Pact was mentioned and applied in some cases. Also, now all of our committees and groups of friends, to whom the preservation of world treasures is dear, should immediately draw the attention of the public to the importance and urgency of the protection of the creations of human genius. Each one of us has certain opportunities of spreading this panhuman idea. Everyone who has connections with the press or who is a member of some cultural organization should consider it his duty to say, wherever he can, a good and impressive word about the defense of that on which the evolution of humanity is based. On March 24 this year, our committee undertook a series of steps imploring European governments to consider without delay the need of defending cultural treasures. We see now that such an appeal was most timely. Let every cultural worker remember now all of his connections and possibilities in order to strengthen, by all means, public opinion, which is first of all the guardian of world treasures. Friends, act urgently.

September 5, 1939

WELCOME TO YOUNGEST FRIENDS!

[*Mira: East & West.* Hyderabad, Vol. V, No. 7,
November, 1939, pp. 788–791]

"HOW do you do, Dr. Lukins:
"You do not know me, but I know you,
although I have not seen you. Auntie told me that you
are President of the Latvian Roerich Society. I too am
his friend; he did not see me either. I am Serge Vitol,
and I am seven and a half years old. And I wish you
would make a society for children only, not to babble,
but to learn how to live better and to be good. I wanted
to come to you, but I cannot because I am going to Lith-
uania. I live there. I will come back in March and shall
come to see you, and then I shall communicate to you
a great secret.

"Yours respectfully, Serge Vitol."

Thus writes our young friend Serge Vitol to the
President of our Latvian Society, Dr. Lukins. And
Dr. Lukins, with his usual all-embracingness and
goodness, remarks that we must also be prepared for
such requirements. When I recollect the multitude of
statements of similar nature from known and unknown
friends, then, verily, we must without delay fulfill this
noble desire of the young seekers for the betterment of
life. Let us then pay firm attention to the words pronounced by Serge Vitol, "Not to babble but to live better." This is the same vital formula of which we adults
always dream, and which again and again is dissolved
in aimless and sterile babbling, prattle, and gossip.

How wonderful it will be if our young friends manifest firm striving in quest of "how to live better." Notice our friend does not speak of entertainment, of having a good time, but he speaks of the betterment of life. He comes, thus, simply to the question of the necessity for the betterment of life. And this simplicity is permeated with the vitality that can revivify any arid desert. Although I do not know personally this young friend, I feel that he will not be satisfied with games nor with our vulgar conception of a kindergarten, where, instead of a positive prognosis, the germs of prejudice are so often being enrooted. Our friend, and all other young friends whom we know, aspire to have a real Society for the betterment of life. He wishes to have serious work; for, as I have already mentioned before, the young ones try to execute with especial care the work entrusted to them by the elder. Even in the household, the young ones participate deeply and seriously in the commissions given to them. We remember with what unusual care five-year-old Olaf set the table, even getting up on a chair in order to better see from above whether everything was in its place. And what zeal seven-year-old Vladimir manifested in cleaning a rifle, because he was entrusted not with a toy gun but with a real gun. And how Allen loved the paintings and had long conversations with them about matters most serious. And how little Jerome tried to introduce in his preparatory class the principle of lawful statesmanship. An endless number of examples can be quoted showing the true and thoughtful cooperation of young friends. I do not forget that my painting for the Kansas City Museum was acquired through a subscription of schoolchildren and that the painting itself was chosen by their vote. And the painting selected was *The Lord*—the expectation of the arrival of the Supreme Lord.

Does this not reflect the inner realization of Hierarchy within our young friends? This most precious conception of creativeness, which later on so often soils and evaporates.

In one assembly of young friends, the project for a city of the Future was discussed. One of the participants of the assembly stated that his city would have no prisons; another said that his city would begin with the erection of a hospital; the third aspired to have a Temple in the center of his city; a fourth had roof gardens in mind; another made a project of special roofs for the landing of airplanes. None of those present at this assembly thought of vaudevilles and vulgar entertainments so dear to the hearts of adults. Have in mind, however, that these participants were not at all anemic pessimists but were strong, happy, and joyous. But neither golf nor fistic smashing of jaws nor vulgar beaches were included in the dreams of the young.

I have seen innumerable children's designs. Except for a few, which were obviously the results of the influences of family surroundings, I never saw one malicious caricature or one mean subject. I recollect how little Stefani depicted the story of Joan of Arc; I recollect fantastic cities, flowers, and animals. I remember various collections. I recollect essays of five- and six-year-old children about expeditions and their observations in the Field of Natural History, about the discovery of new lands, stars, and a new sun. I recollect whole books, which were written during the first school years, on ornithology, dendrology, and mineralogy. I remember very artistic and instructive postcard collections that, in contrast to those of adults, did not include any vulgar subjects, which often are published in such profusion as though at the demand of the masses. Let us remember the theatres arranged by young friends with all adoptions so that they should be like a real theatre. I remember how once a young friend, having invited his playmates to visit him, distributed among them his toy soldiers, but he set himself down with a book to read. In answer, to everyone's astonishment, he said, "Let them be busy if they are interested, and I will read in the meanwhile." During the construction of a model fleet, the ships with their many sails are not always directed to war, but on the contrary, they carry important news, discover new lands, transport new machinery, or defend their own shores.

Penetrating into the self-development of the consciousness of our young friends, we find an endless multitude of facts and comparisons that give deep joy. If the distorted conceptions of life would not obscure the development of these consciousnesses, how many true possibilities of progress would be created, and how much of the vulgar and mean would disappear from life.

Many a time, an adult, through a light-minded and foolish attitude toward the foundations of life and religion, diverts forever the worthy striving instinct of the younger generation. Sometimes, in an unjust accusation, a child's mother makes the pretense of consulting God, and Oh horror! This God gives an unjust verdict, and, under the eyes of the young ones, the church is transformed into a club. As though it would pass unnoticed by the young eyes! But vigilant are the eyes of the young, and they notice much that later on, perhaps, might slip attention. The absorption of the first years is more intense than that of the following years.

Dear Serge, you have a kind aunt who gave you the address of Dr. Lukins. Dear Serge—and you all— you have variously manifested your hearty and serious intentions! We shall, in every way, encourage your societies with the aim of "how to live better." We shall consider it our joy when our friends learn to open the glorious Gates. We shall rejoice with you if you find the joy of creative labor and if you realize the power of thought.

You speak about your secrets, but the secret of your heart is not destructive. It is constructive and benevolent. You desire to know of the good, and you intend to go toward it by the shortest and straightest way. This good will be vouchsafed to you; if you will reach it in full and radiant faith, this immutable knowledge will lead you to the Good, to the Beautiful, which is crowned by the one, all-conquering Light! It shall be a day of joy to receive news from your societies that strive to the Good! Thus shall we enrich the store of our joys. Let us affirm ourselves in the joy of creative labor, in the joy of cooperation, in the joy of cognizance, and in all joys that will lead us to the great realization of Culture.

GOOD SPEED!

[*The Scholar*. Palghat, Vol. XV, No. 5,
February, 1940, pp. 197-199]

ALMOST a hundred years ago, the celebrated Russian author Gogol, amid his remarkable letters and addresses to friends, wrote the following unfading thoughts:

I see and hear all; your sufferings are great. For one with such a delicate soul to endure such gross accusation; with such exalted feelings, to live in the midst of such coarse, loutish people, such as the dwellers of the commonplace, small town in which you have taken up your abode; whose one unfeeling, gross contact is vigorously to smash the best heart's treasure, even without knowing it. To strike with the paw of a bear upon the most refined chords of the soul, which have been given for singing out heavenly sounds—to disrupt and to wring contempt from the despised—all this is grievous, I know. Your bodily sufferings are no less burdensome. Your nervous ailments, the anguish by which you are now possessed—all this is heavy, ponderous, and I can say nothing more to you than only, grievous! But here is consolation for you. This is only the beginning; there will be still more affronts to you. You will still engage in the severest struggles with scoundrels of all sorts and with shameless people for whom nothing is sacred; who not only promote that odious matter about which you write, i.e., signing a strange name; to dare to impute a most frightful offense to an innocent soul; to see with one's own eyes, chastisement striking at the slandered one and not to shudder; not only a similar, odious matter but others many times more heinous, about which a single narrative can forever deprive of sleep a compassionate man. Better for these people not to be born at all! The whole host of Heavenly Forces shudders at the horror of the punishment beyond the grave awaiting them, from which no one can deliver them. You will encounter countless new and entirely unexpected blows. Anything may happen to your almost defenseless career. Your nervous attacks and ailments also will become still more severe; your anguish will be more deadly and your sorrows more devastating. But remember, not at all have we been called into the world for picnics and feasting—to battle have we been summoned hither; we shall celebrate the victory there. And, therefore, we ought not to forget for an instant that we have entered the fray, and it is not for us, here, to select a place of lesser danger; as a good warrior, each one should rush thither where the battle is hottest. On high, the heavenly Captain looks over us all, and not the least matter escapes His gaze. Do not shirk the field of battle, but, having drawn near to the fight, seek out a strong enemy, not a weak one. For fighting with small grief and little afflictions, you do not receive much glory. Forward then, my excellent warrior! With God, good comrade! With God, my excellent friend! (1846)

Of course, this was said by an imaginary person in a play by Gogol, himself the writer, the thinker. He was one who had the right to say, "I see."

We do not quote from the *Exhortation of Gogol* for the reason that his book happens to be at hand. It is not as if this volume has been casually purchased wherein Lomonosov and Derzhavin are also significantly spoken about. Not by accident has come with us through Chinese and Mongolian lands the Russian searcher of hearts, "I see and hear all." For a long time, this fellow traveler has been close by; "therefore, let us go and see and hear."

"I see and hear all." If someone is only slightly concerned, he will not hear everything. He may not know how to hear. If one has developed within himself this capability in good, in courage, and steadfastness, then he distinctly fixes different degrees of hearing, but it is possible both to hear all and to find a place for everything. Gogol, who described conflict so remarkably, who went through all the hardships of life to the great and luminous, knew that the knowledge of dangers is guarding in advance against fear. Preparation for the worst will always provide the possibility of intensifying the special forces. Many are the forces in man; it only is necessary to draw them out of their repository in good time. Such storehouses are deep, and the entries to them are complicated. It is possible to study the locks upon them in company with the great (guides? Vedantists?). One needs to be assured of these great fellow travelers. One needs to feel that he will not be exhorted into anything wrong, and then it is easy to proceed; then all illusory obstacles resolve themselves into a peculiar pattern.

Between fellow travelers, there will be no ugly thoughts; the abusive word is entirely excluded as vestiges of the animals' roar. It is very important that fellow wayfarers should not, even casually, make use of filthy names among themselves. Let us not demand love, immediately, which does not come so easily, but mutual respect on the path is indispensable.

In caravans, one can observe how sometimes by following people's thoughts and feelings, the animals themselves imitate their conduct. One has had occasion to end feelings; the animals themselves imitate their conduct. One has had occasion to see how at the irritation of people, up until that time friendly, the dogs hurled themselves at each other, and the horses and camels took fright. Such a graphic indication, about which experienced caravanners distinctly know, should remain in the memory of all fellow travelers.

This fellow wayfarer is already a coworker, yet this coworker has not been accidentally encountered. Joint action remains inevitable. It stays somewhere forever. The inexperienced think, "Let us separate and all will be ended." But the matter is not altogether thus. Even on the purely material plane, you see how boomerangs return. He who acts in conscious responsibility already understands that by each action is tomorrow's day being forged.

An enemy of the human race invented all forms of intoxication. In it is contained loss of responsibility. What ugly accumulations result from any intoxication? Therefore, fellow wayfarers are temperate.

People remember that "you go for a day but take bread for a week." This has been said as a result of large experience; verily, of any kind of bread one needs to take a seven-fold quantity. Likewise, wisdom enjoins that parting is more joyful than meeting. Of course, meeting presupposes parting, yet each parting already forebodes meeting. And on what paths the meeting will be, let us not concern ourselves, provided the paths be those of good.

Gogol, in all his sincere aspirations, nevertheless speaks about the battle. No other name is fitting. But Kurukshetra is also battle. All peoples know such battles, for in no other wise can you call this advancement. When, then, the heart will be maintained outside of any intoxications, it will very subtly give one the sign as to where the front is being established good and strong.

"Forward, then, my excellent warrior."

And from ancient times sounds the call of the

Anguttara Nikāya to the same spiritual battle: "Warriors, warriors, we call ourselves. We fight for noble virtue, for lofty effort, for sublime wisdom; for this reason, we call ourselves warriors!"

WORMS

[*The Scholar.* Palghat, Vol. XV, No. 6,
March, 1940, pp. 235–237]

ALL kinds of injuries are contained in foul speech. In each noxious speaking can be found all abominable and shameful vices. Each evil speech contains in itself hatred, falsehood, treachery, and all that which so impedes the well-being of humanity.

Even if ignorance lies at the base of all these vices, this still makes it no easier for the contemporary consciousness. What profound turpitude is contained in any treachery, in each falsehood, in slander, and in a desire to injure one's fellow. Long ago, these vices were placed in a group of the most abominable, bestial manifestations.

The Apostle Paul, in his first epistle to Timothy, places falsehood, slander, and perjury in the series of the following loathsome manifestations.

"Know ye that the law has been established not for the righteous but for the lawless and the unruly, the impious and the sinful, the corrupt and the profane, the offenders against father and mother, for murderers.

"For lechers, sodomites, kidnappers, slanderers, human beasts, liars, perjurers, and all the others who are opposed to sound doctrine."

You see in what a shameful list has been included liars, slanderers, and all spoilers. And yet how easy it is amid contemporary civilization to utter falsehood, slander, treachery, and all that can arrest the growth of useful things. There has even been spoken about a selflessness of evil, which in its violence actually reaches the point of self-abnegation. There are those who are prepared even to smite themselves provided they can sow evil.

Of course, it is so easy to perform any treachery. Sometimes people do not even render themselves on account that by a word or deed they destroy that very thing with which yesterday they were in agreement and which they served. Some small evil-speaking has taken place; it may be from external irritation, or it may be from some deeply concealed thoughts. Yet, here, these apparently small causes incite a man to begin to commit treachery even though therein he harms himself.

Indeed, each treachery, first of all, rebounds back upon the evil speaker himself, as does each falsehood and slander. This remains an immutable truth. But it makes it no easier for the well-being of people, the fact that any traitor or slanderer receives what he deserves. Nevertheless, the places overgrown by the weeds of evil speech require much effort in order to clean them up again.

Indeed, evil speech does not fall from heaven. It is begotten in the lowest strata of life. It grows slowly but inexorably, if only it be sown. At first, the man learns to smile evilly, to shrug his shoulders evilly, then to utter the evil jest; he is elated by the irritation or the approbation of his companion, and, then, imperceptibly he becomes accustomed to the basest evil-speaking.

Evil speech, the same as invective, is first of all a vicious habit. The Apostle was absolutely right in placing falsehood and slander in the list of offenses contrary to nature. In the eyes of civilized society, any of the vices named by him are manifestly inadmissible. But not so with slander and treachery. Certainly, they have not been expelled from the way of life, like bestiality. And, of course, all this testifies identically to a beastly state.

Noxious insects breed from filth and negligence. From such carelessness are also born the worms of treachery. People are advised not to feed dogs raw meat. From raw meat, worms appear in them, which are sometimes very difficult to get rid of. Are there not contained in meat food all those grossnesses of life that are so injurious? Are not the worms of slander and treachery bred from the same causes as in the case of dogs?

Sometimes people attempt to explain treacherous and slanderous actions by small-souledness. In the last analysis, what is the smallness of soul? After all, there certainly is the seed of the spirit in everyone. But it can become covered with dust and relegated into the cellars of the consciousness. Then, it is more accurate to say, not small-souledness but mean-souledness. And this vice will also not be entirely natural but will be engendered in the ugliness of a moldy way of life.

The infectiousness of vices can be observed even in the smallest of them. In any group, one has but to fall in with one or another vice to which one is attracted, and sooner or later one becomes a follower of it. Sometimes such an inwardly prepared follower will even condemn the vicious qualities observed by them. But, then, little by little he will catch the pernicious habits. It is striking to observe how gradually a vicious habit takes root. Undoubtedly, the man is ashamed of it. At first, he unfailingly tries to conceal it; but later, seeing obvious examples of it and noticing that those surrounding him do not all change their attitude toward him, he wears his odious habit outwardly. And so, no matter, he continues to dwell in a human-like society.

All kinds of worms exist. Physicians affirm that certain of them are extremely difficult to eradicate, and their return is always possible. But no organism is wormy from the beginning. These vipers insinuate themselves very gradually, from envy, from self-pity, from stupidity, and, in general, from ignorance

These pernicious worms are not spoken about in schools. They may be discussed only when they have appeared in some unseemly behavior. But, of course, then it will be too late. Then a prophylaxis is not required but some special measures of taking unpleasant remedies. The majority of people are very careful about their taste and do not like bad-tasting medicines. If a physician prescribes them, such people will try to consign these medicaments to the trash bin. It is better not to acquire the worms than to contend with them later.

There exists a terrible malady, the final stage at which all the pores of the body begin to give out worms. It is said that King Herod ended his life in such a fetid dissolution. Yet in each breath, the stubborn traitor and slanderer exhale these same horrible worms, in their invisibility still more dangerous.

Yes, in the case of dogs, worms are acquired from raw meat; from some such raw meat are bred the human worms that infect the whole surrounding atmosphere. From such meat, people reach such a state of torpor that they lose the faculty of distinguishing colors, and they cannot listen to and understand the simplest things. Is this not from cannibalism?

In dogs, worms are acquired from raw meat. From where then comes that human grossness that reaches such a state of ravenousness that even the most steadfast ties find themselves broken. From very imperceptible vulgarities and meannesses are the human worms propagated. The example of the worm-eater King Herod has been noted down in history. Not without cause has the animal-like state of Nebuchadnezzar also been related. People try to avoid and to destroy rats that are the bearers of contagion. Then what about worms, both visible and invisible?

NEITHER DAY NOR HOUR

[*The Jatri.* Calcutta, April–May, 1944, pp. 5770–5773]

RANDOM riding is an excellent exercise. At all times, the rider is in an intensely attentive state. Not only must he be prepared for the most unexpected command, but he must also keep his horse in the same readiness. Acquiring preparedness will mean that an attentive and solicitous eye will be kept open throughout life. If testing of preparedness were carried out in different aspects in all educational institutions, this would create entire cadres of people, mobile and healthy in consciousness.

"Always be prepared"—this beautiful motto of the Boy Scouts expresses the wish to be ready at all times. But of course, apart from the wish, one must be tested in preparedness. One should know how to apply this quality under any and all circumstances.

There must be readiness for the most highly diverse actions. There must be readiness for patience. There must be readiness for endurance. There must be readiness for clear decisions in the most dissimilar and contrasting circumstances.

Often people understand preparedness only as it regards outward actions. But, of course, this is only one part of the consciousness of true preparedness. Man must prove himself both in speech and in silence, not only in movement and tumult but also in silent motionlessness of the body. Man must learn preparedness, not only in circumstances that are agreeable to him but also he must prove himself among precisely such condition as through chance habits he does not like. Of course, he cannot justify any failure of his by the fact that the conditions of action did not conform to his previously formed habits.

This tense state of preparedness frees people forever from boredom. After all, what is boredom? Primarily, this will be a lack of knowledge of how to employ the time that one has on one's hands. With boredom, a person begins to fall into thoughtlessness or to give himself over to preconceived ideas. But, surely, each moment of life can be employed for discerning something undeferrably useful, and in this feeling of usefulness, boredom will be eliminated.

Each one has had occasion to observe absurd arguments, such as this—that to one only rubies are pleasing, while another talks only about emeralds and is delighted by them alone. Such senseless disputes only create an oppressive atmosphere. Let one be attracted to rubies and let the other be charmed by emeralds. But if the *ruby* man has to die in order to appreciate the beautiful radiance of the emerald, then he will simply be unprepared for broad perceptions. Likewise, precisely the limitedness of the *emerald* man brings him only grief in life. All natural colors are beautiful, each one in its refraction and its scintillation. One may have a secret predisposition for certain mineral, color, and sound. But apart from this possible innate predilection, one must cultivate an appreciation for all the other beauties.

One man believes that he finds an enraptured frame of mind in feasting his eyes upon the glitter of Venus. Another feels that the magnetic secret of Orion gives him inspiration. A third is fascinated by contemplation of the Pole Star or the Great Bear, while yet another dreams about the constellation of the Southern Cross. There are many profound reasons for this. But he who admires Orion or is inspired by the Southern Cross will be in a very insignificant state of preparedness if he does not find within himself the joy of all the other heavenly abodes.

All of this would seem very simple and well understood. But why, then, in their everyday life, do people display such a shameful lack of preparedness, of receptivity to broad perceptions? Let there burn deeply in one's heart a dream about the constellation of the Three Magi; but in this, let one not belittle a feeling of rapture toward the Seven Elders. For some reason, the same constellation will remind one person about the Great Bear and another about the Seven Elders. Such a distinction of mode does not at all exclude joy about the same constellation. Thus, there are many joys. Only one must have the preparedness to perceive them and to live by them.

If someone shall deny the unquestionable beauties of nature for the mere purpose of limiting himself to one single particle of them, he simply shows how many lessons in preparedness he still has to learn. Each one has encountered so many narrow specialists who could think only about one almost infinitesimal particle of existence. Of course, in the last analysis, they only inspire regret for the obvious fact that they have simply not happened to be in contact with a great number of others so that they could realize commensurateness. One would like to toss them into a set of completely unaccustomed conditions and say to them, "Now then, brother, swim out." Then would ensue great testing; many would feel themselves victims of misfortune and would fall into dire straits. But as for those in whom the inner chalice was already full, they would fetch out of it everything applicable to the given situation, and instead of failure, they would create still another success and joy.

Any creating of joy is a strengthening and a flowering of existence. Let the deserts of the spirit blossom where there is the capacity to cause joy to burst forth. The deeper the roots of this joy shall be, the more flowery and fruitful will be the transformation of the desert.

Need one make haste? May it be that any impetuous haste in infinity will be senseless? Yet when you consider the velocities existing in space, you can then understand how much celerity of the spirit will always be timely and proper. Preparedness lies precisely in the consciousness, in the spirit. Therefore, the cultivation of preparedness also must, first of all, take place in spiritual cognition. And the potential of the swiftness of the spirit, of the speed of thought, fully conforms to spatial velocities.

Any ignorant limitation directly contradicts infinity. Therefore, each hour of earthly life must be filled with strivings in order to conform, though relatively, to infinity.

Indeed, much will appear practically incommensurate. But in the spirit material, standards do not exist, and, therefore, the most extreme measures of preparedness will be simply the true path.

Let no one think that the bustle of the marketplace is a good example of preparedness. Of course, such bustling is very superficial, but the agitation of the ocean is not at all measured by the surface movements of the waters. These fleeting waves do not make difficult the progress of the vessel. But the deep, mountainous rolling of the ocean can destroy the strongest rigged ship.

When undeferrable preparedness is spoken about, precisely well-timed is the reminder, "neither day nor hour." The sojourn here is so brief that each moment must be filled up, both outwardly and, principally, inwardly.

What joy it is to feel both containment and preparedness. Of course, preparedness without containment will still be far from full. In this developed sensitiveness, one can discern where is the true possibility and where is an actual irreparable danger. There are few bodily dangers in comparison with the many spiritual perils. A true husbandman always keeps the water supplies of his home in a state of cleanliness. He knows that if he does not have a daily look at the sources, the rubbish of everyday life will undoubtedly foul them. Whether this dust be brought in by the wind or through someone's malicious or ignorant will, corrupt products will be cast into the source; no matter which, caring for the source must be continuous.

Constantly twinkling fires are fatiguing to the eyes. They are harmful to the eyesight. Likewise injurious are spasms, convulsions, and paroxysms. But still more damage is done by the paroxysms and convulsions of moods. These twinkling fires are not suitable for construction. Even light, inextinguishable and growing, completely illumines all the possibilities of labors. There will be no bewildering twilights during which malignant destroyers obtain entrance.

Great preparedness is required for kindling an inextinguishable light. Each hour of the day and half the night, this light does not permit the dark destroyers to draw near. It is no abstraction that this lamp of the heart must be guarded and preserved.

A man may fall, as it were, into an empty place. If he be limited and spasmodic, he falls into dejection and, thus, proves himself worthless. He will try mentally to plant this place with his prejudices grown elsewhere. But whoever is ready for building, whoever strives consciously and invincibly, will inspect the mirage of the empty place and may find that precisely here great events have taken place, full of instructive possibilities. The place will be empty only for the unprepared in spirit. But in preparedness, in unbreakable zeal, does man bring life into the deserts.

It is said, "If thou art tired, begin again. If thou art exhausted, begin again and again."

THE MONGOLS

[*The Scholar.* Palghat, Vol. XV, No. 11,
August, 1940, pp. 443–447]

THE banner of Chengiz Khan was white. In different campaigns, he used various symbols—the lion, the steed of happiness, the falcon, or the panther. Fundamentally, the color of the Mongols is blue.

The laws of the Great Khan are extant even to this day, and we may recall many that are applicable to our present life. His severe penalties for theft, murder, adultery, and other offenses could be placed upon the pages of our law even in the present times. Similarly, with his other official acts, his orders to his officers and his steps for the progress of his country were broadly introduced by the Great Khan.

In order to prevent pride and vanity among the khans, Chengiz Khan forbade the adoption of pompous titles. Freedom of religion and speech were observed and the love of God acknowledged. Clergy and physicians were freed from public taxes. Capital punishment was prescribed for spies, perjurers, sorcerers, and those who accepted bribes. The marriage laws forbade marriage between the next of kin. And to raise the sense of honor, it was forbidden to employ one's next of kin as servants. To abolish intoxication, Chengiz Khan constantly discountenanced the use of strong beverages and urged his people to eliminate the use of these entirely.

A regulation is also known to have aimed at the abolishing of excessive superstitions. The ordinances of Chengiz Khan encouraged hospitality among his nomad population and insured the safety of travelers throughout the vast extent of his empire. Rules were given in regard to campsites, and divisions of *yurtas* were made into tens, hundreds, and thousands.

Along the caravan routes, military stations with guards were established, and at intervals of a day's journey, posts for horses were set. The army was divided into divisions of tens, hundreds, thousands, and ten thousands. Capital punishment was meted out to all officers who deserted their posts.

Judging by everything that has come down to us, Chengiz Khan was a great leader and organizer.

"The Lord preserve us from the Mongols!" Such were the inscriptions found in destroyed cities of Asia. Danish fishermen did not venture into the open sea for fear of a Mongolian invasion.

This is one of the earliest descriptions of the Mongols, presented to Europe in the thirteenth century, which was created by fear and terror:

Lest human joys be especially prolonged, and the world's benevolence endure too long without tears [wrote Matthew Peris in the year 1240], reviling creatures of Satan himself, the countless Tartar hordes broke loose and swept out of the boundaries of their encampments surrounded by mountains. Swarming like locust over the earth, they brought terrible devastation to Western Europe, and by fire and sword reduced it to a wasteland. They are inhuman, bestial, more monsters than men. They thirst for blood and gorge themselves with it. They rend and devour dogs and human flesh, and dress in skins with their chests and backs naked except for armor. They are small in stature, stocky, hairy, invincible. With zest they drink the pure blood of their herds. Their horses are stout, strong, and eat branches, and even trees. Due to their short thighs, they have to mount these horses with the aid of three-stepped ladders. . . . They know no laws; they are completely lacking in any idea of comfort and are more ferocious than lions or bears. . . . they have pity neither for age nor sex nor position. . . . they know no language to converse in besides their own, which no one understands, because up to recent times there was no contact with them, and they themselves never came beyond the boundaries of their country. Thus, there is no information available about their customs and personalities, such as is gained through the mutual intercourse of people. They travel with their herds and wives, and the latter are accustomed to fight as well as the men. To the destruction of Christendom, they suddenly appear, and with the speed of lightning ravage and annihilate everything on their way, terrorizing everyone, and arousing terrific hatred everywhere.

This was the reputation of the Mongols when their name first reached Europe, accompanied by the sensational terror that usually preceded their attacks. The very word Tartar aroused terror; they were considered the scourge of God. The old writers called them the "plague of God"—demons sent against men in punishment.

Europe did not regard the Mongols as human beings. It denied them the honor of being enemies or customary adversaries and considered them some sort of superhuman creatures. In those times, Europeans sincerely believed that Mongols had dogs' heads and devoured human flesh. This was the sort of wild terror that gripped Europe before the appearance of the Tartars. The danger that threatened humanity was regarded as so extreme that even Danish fishermen did not venture into the open sea for fear of Mongols.

The same picture is apparent at that time within the boundary of the Far East as well as in the Far West—on the shores of the Pacific as well as on shores of the Black Sea. One of the Chinese historians of that period exclaims with dismay that "since the creation of the world, no nation has been as powerful as the present Mongols. They devastate entire countries more easily than we pluck grass. Why do the heavens permit it?"

Another writer, describing the consequences of Mongolian supremacy, significantly remarks that "in Asia and Western Europe a dog can hardly bark without the permission of the Mongols."

After overwhelming all Asia, and reaching the threshold of Europe, the Mongolian invasion seemed such an ominous threat that the rulers of Europe began frantically to take council with each other as to ways of meeting the threatening danger. It was decided to undertake united resistance against this human deluge, as no single country could cope with it alone. No proof is more evident of the fear that these Mongol hordes inspired, even within the limits of the greatest European countries of that period, than the call of Frederick II, Holy Roman Emperor, to the entire Christian world to repel the invasion of the dreaded Mongols. Just imagine an appeal addressed to "Germany, ardent in battles; France, nursing at her bosom a fearless army; militant Spain; England, powerful in men and ships; Crete; Sicily; wild Hibernia; and cold Norway," asking them to organize international crusades against the nomad conquerors who came to Europe from far-off Mongolia.

Excerpts from the manifesto of Frederick II eloquently describe the *Mongol Terror* that surrounded Europe in 1240:

These people [wrote the Emperor] have emerged from the far ends of the world, where they have long been concealed in an atmosphere of terrific climatic extremities and have suddenly and brutally swept upon the Northern countries, swarming like locusts. No one knows whence this fierce race has gained its title of Tartar, but one thing is certain, it is apparently God's Will that this race has been preserved from prehistoric days as a weapon to scourge people for their transgressions, and mayhap even for the fall of Christendom. This brutal, savage people has not the least conception of humane principles. They have a leader whom they revere, and whose command they blindly obey, calling him the earthly god. They are small in stature, stocky, strong with great resistance, and have unbreakable faith. At the least sign from their leader, they throw themselves with reckless valor against the most incredible perils. They have broad faces, slanting eyes, and emit the most terrifying shrieks and outcries, which indicate vividly the savagery of their hearts. They know no other raiment except the skins of oxen, asses, and horses, and up to now their armor is only crudely and badly soldered iron plates. But now—and we cannot mention this without a shudder—they begin to improve their armor by looting that of the Christians. Soon the Lord's wrath will descend on all of us, and these barbarians will begin to kill us, to our shame, with our own weapons. The Tartars already are learning to dress richly and elaborately, and at present they eat the most savory food. They ride beautiful horses and are inimitable archers. It is said that their horses when they have no other fodder, eat foliage, bark, and roots of trees, and yet preserve their courage, strength, and agility.

Thus, Europe estimated the Mongol conquerors.

In later times, these estimates become more exact and more detailed. For instance, Timur, instead of the former evaluation of a destroyer, received from the French savant Grousset a completely different estimate. Grousset says that Timur "who combines the subtle strivings of Iranian-Hindu culture with the austere mold of an ascetic, appears as one of the most colorful figures of the Indo-Iranian world." Thus, the great son of Chengiz Khan in the clan of Barlass is presented in a new light by the reflective scientist Grousset. Similarly, many rulers of the world, who were hastily condemned, as quickly revealed themselves in a completely different light. Is this not the case in Russian History with Ivan the Terrible and Peter the Great?

In recalling the description of Grousset and the notes of Plano Karpini about the interest in arts and sciences of Mongolia, we may consider that the Mongolian apotheosis reached the zenith in Akbar the Great. Of course, there have been prejudiced judgments of him as a bloodthirsty tyrant, but there has finally emerged a brilliant picture of the resplendent unifier and cultured ruler of a great country. And to this luminous image of Akbar, already apparent, new studies can only add new valuable signs. And the wisdom of the people, which is just at its base, will add the aureole of a saint to the image of the Great Emperor. Thus through the centuries, people can revere a consistently great service. In regard to the characteristics of Mongols, I also recall other notes by contemporaneous travelers. There are many valuable and benevolent tokens. One should likewise remember the sacred Mongolian books, with their covenants about the Bodhisattvas, and their admonitions to compassion, self-sacrifice, and help to one's neighbor. Let us also recall the Nestorian times. In short, let us not in any way disparage that which was so real a factor in the life of this strong and courageous people.

How many beautiful hours we recall from our own travels in Mongolia. I remember the hearty greeting of welcome of the Mongol Rin-chin. How much we valued also the fiery exclamation of the gray-headed Buriat, "Light conquers darkness!" I remember how valiantly the Mongols acted in our encounter with bandits. I remember the building of the *suburgan* and the gracious offering of their treasures. If we go by the marks of benevolence, we will find many of them. No matter how often a nation finds rebirth, its foundations still prevail. The same may be observed with many other peoples. Circumstances may change, bringing happiness or ill-fortune, but the soul of the people remains. And one may trace this folk-soul by its ancient songs, its sayings, and its parables. In these indestructible folk mementos, one can find the worthiest characteristics.

In the laws of the Mongolian Khans, in the heroic epic of these people, is reflected a nature that is firm, courageous, often ascetic, patiently enduring the vicissitudes of their time.

And perceiving these covenants of the past, which have not been lost in the currents of the present day, should we not help these people who desire peaceful progress?

There was a time when the circumstances of life and the yearnings of their heart enticed the Mongols into far-off places because man often thinks that the beyond is more alluring—splendid are the drums beyond the mountains." But contemporary thought has directed the Mongols toward the treasures of their own lands. To appreciate our own possessions, to learn to evaluate that which is defined by destiny, is a great accomplishment. It so happens that the Mongols as such, having concerned themselves with remote places, did not as yet exhaust their own inner treasures. Not to use means not to waste. Therefore, it is but just to direct attention to Mongolia with benevolence and friendship.

No one will make the error of exclaiming again, "Lord preserve us from the Mongols." On the contrary, thoughtful persons will send hearty wishes for the peaceful regeneration of their people.

Rigden Djepo himself, in resplendent armor, is galloping on. The Mongols do not forget the visions of the Great Lama in 1927. So it is also said in the prophecies:

"On the slope toward the sunrise, a white stone will be revealed with an inscription. . . . and though you hew out this inscription, it will never disappear but will forever emerge again."

THE THREE SWORDS

[*The Twentieth Century*. Allahabad, July–August, 1943, p. 499]

THE *Wooden Sword*—The ancient Ostrov in the Pskov Province, on the river Velikaya and the fortress on the island! In 1879, we visited our grandmother, Tatiana Ivanovna Korkunov-Kalashnikov. At Lipenka there was an old house with a large garden, run wild. The first floor was of white stone; the upper floor and the attic were of wood, painted in ochre, and the shutters and window frames were painted white.

Beneath flowed the Velikaya, and behind was a park belonging to a large estate, with a white house in the style of Catherine.

There were bushes full of berries and burdock in my grandmother's garden, and I wanted to fight with these dragons but had no sword. In the neighborhood, however, was one Ivan Ivanovich Chugunov, a building contractor, who had all sorts of workmen. Things have a way of getting around, for he heard of my desire and brought in a brand-new wooden sword. It was well made with a long blade, and the hilt was carved. My only regret was that it was made of the wood of the linden tree, yet it was painted to look like bronze. All the same, I decided that it would serve my purpose, and many dragons were laid low in my grandmother's garden.

The Iron Sword—1896. The Academy of Arts. The idea of painting the suite *Slavonic Russia* was projected while other pictures, such as: *The Messenger, Uprising of the Tribes,*

Meeting of the Elders, The Campaign, and *Building of the Town* were executed.

I read much history. At Izvara an old chicken house was converted into a studio.

I began collecting wolf and lynx skins. The Slavs also had to have arms. A village blacksmith, covered with soot, forged a real iron sword for me made to resemble those found in the Kurgans. For a long time, this sword hung in the storeroom. George remembers it.

The Fiery Sword—1913. The fiery sword is brought to the sleeping sentinels. My painting the *Sword of Courage* is now a necessity. The dates are being fulfilled. At the beginning of 1914, *The Red Dawn* (with the Belgian Lion), *The Cry of the Serpent, The Crowns* (disappearing in the clouds), *Human Deeds,* and *The Doomed City* were hastily executed, together with all those pictures whose meaning we only understood later.

The *Fiery Sword* is for the threshold of a New World. And now, in 1939, we recall these three swords.

In Western Tibet, three swords have been carved on the rocks from time immemorial. The boundary? Victory? The symbol of the three swords comes to memory.

The Sword of Courage!

PARALLEL THINKING

[*The Dawn of India.* Calcutta, Vol. V, No. 10, May, 1944, p. 648]

MUCH has been said about priority and imitation, but certain causes of simultaneous ideas have been overlooked. In all fields of art and science, one may be convinced of similar manifestations. One cannot impute imitation or plagiarism to people whose geographical position prevented their knowing of identical or similar developments. In the history of art, there are cases when almost identical compositions of the human figure appear in revivified forms of an art long past and unknown to the author. One could fill a large volume with examples of a most varied character. There have been cases when an artist was astonished to find in some remote work of art, the very forms that he had already conceived within himself. The artist would be sincere in saying that he had never seen such a production. The Sceptic, of course, would reply that he had probably seen it somewhere but forgotten it. We must not exclude such cases of forgetfulness. Art forms often emerge from the consciousness where they have long been deposited. Today, however, in this age of radio waves and thought transmission, we can discern other reasons for parallel thinking. Such unexpected manifestations are analogous ideas, and conceptions are carried by the radio waves of space, and people of similar receptivity pick them up in the most remote corners of the globe. Not so long ago, this analogy of the power of thought would have been considered as a fable. Recent scientific achievements, however, convince us that apart from imitation or plagiarism, similar forms can appear at different times in different countries. Artists, writers, scholars—all confirm the fact that they are often absorbed by identical problems. This is proof of parallel thinking and one to which we should devote serious thought. Space is filled with ideas and conceptions.

REMAINS

[*The Dawn of India*. Calcutta, Vol. V, No. 8,
March, 1944, pp. 571-572]

THE whole world is now obsessed with the writing of memoirs. It might seem that this circumstance would be an advantage for the future historian. But is it going to work that way? When you begin to compare different memoirs dealing with the same events, you are struck by their discordances. If this is so today, one may ask what the situation will be like when there are only reminiscences. We are apt to think that large encyclopedias and reference books are the most reliable. I pick up the Encyclopedia Britannica, which has passed through many editions. I find errors in it relative to myself and Tibet. If such mistakes exist in matters one is familiar with, then how many mistakes will be found in other sections? We cannot assume that errors appeared simply in this case. The position of the historian is thus made very difficult. Before him lie thick volumes that are considered to carry authority, yet the facts contained in them are often contradictory. One can imagine how chronicles and annals of the past were distorted in passing from lip to lip. When you travel through Central Asia and listen to all the stories picked up by the long Asiatic ear, then you can picture the past, when classic historians had to deal with exactly the same sort of information. There were no sources, save the oral transmission of travelers. It thus happens that along with sound facts there is much fiction, and it is this that amazes you in the accounts of travelers and story-tellers. It is said that in the course of time, history sifts out the truth.

On the mountain trails to Khotan, we saw several caves that once served as retreats for Buddhist anchorites. To reach them from the heights above would be a very complicated undertaking. In caves lower down, one finds the remains of murals, which the Muslims and the campfires of the Kara-Kirghiz have not succeeded in destroying. Besides fanatics, these murals have met with enemies in the form of scientists who "for the sake of science" have cut out whole sections of these frescoes. One large figure of a Bodhisattva, for example, was so cut up that one portion went to London, another to Delhi, while the boots took shelter in Khotan. Besides these enemies, there were mice. In the cellars of the Berlin Museum, many frescoes of which the plaster was made with straw were devoured by mice. The problem is whether to divide up such monuments among museums or to find a means to preserve them just as their creators left them. Who knows whether the desert may not again become a dwelling place? No epithet is too strong to stigmatize those who destroy such monuments. It is sad to see these plundered, half-burned wall decorations in the cave temples. These *frescoes* were not only valuable as art but were documents showing the fusion of Indian and Iranian art, touched with Chinese influences. The contemplation of such ruins fills one with sadness. One feels that if they had been left alone, such monuments would have been an important store in Kharahoto. We recall how one explorer, baffled by many contradictory indications, stopped in despair on the site of an ancient city and decided to try his luck there, with the result that he made a most valuable discovery. Here in the Kulu Valley are said to be hidden some very ancient manuscripts. The tradition is deeply rooted and coincides with the historic iconoclasm of Langdharma. What lucky *chance* may lead to their discovery? According to the accounts of Chinese travelers, there were once fourteen monasteries in this valley. Where are they today?

They have given us a perfect picture of the flowering of art in those places, which the hand of man has turned into barren deserts. The murmur of underground streams reminds us that life-giving moisture has not yet forsaken these spots and that it can be brought forth again to make fruitful these barren sands. The ruins of a cave monastery near Kuchar particularly impressed us. Through a narrow gorge, we fell, as it were, into a broad amphitheater, on the sides of which were many temples and monastic cells. One realized the great antiquity of this place, through which had passed Buddhists, Nestorians, and Manichaeans. The frescoes were almost all broken or defaced, yet one felt how rich the originals must have been. It is not possible now to enter all these caves. When you walk through the upper caves, you gather from the hollow sound that there must be other compartments beneath. It would require much careful engineering to avoid a destructive rockslide. Besides the murals, many sculptured figures adorn this one-time monastery. Now there remain only a few pedestals, which sometimes display fragments of feet. Here, in a spacious cave, was a representation of Parinirvana, and on the narrow cornices between the caves, a row of statues. Below are seen scattered rubble and pieces of building materials. Yet here, through the rubbish peeps a small fragment of frescoes. You feel that this place was once magnificent, filled with people and adorned with love. The dying out of such a center must have been accompanied by many dramas. More than one hostile invasion must have fallen on it. It is fascinating to tap the walls and floor and to speculate about hidden retreats. There are probably whole libraries yet to be discovered. One recalls how in Tun-Huang, a monk discovered, quite by chance, a number of valuable manuscripts.

TO FRIENDS

[*The Dawn of India.* Calcutta, Vol. V, No. 8,
March, 1944, pp. 575-578]

MY dear Friends:
We shall say briefly wherein the substance of
our tasks and striving lies. Everything which is defined
can be expressed briefly: "We are helping Culture." And
if someone in a moment of audacity should take upon
himself the burden of saying, "We are constructing Culture," then he will be not far from the truth. Does not
each one who helps, appear to be a coworker?

We are asking our friends every day to think, to pronounce, and to apply the understanding of Beauty and
Culture. And this is nothing new because there is nothing new anywhere. But we are gathering around these
precious understandings a new effort; we are striving to
help toward the tension of creative energy. We are striving to learn and to reincarnate the so-called abstraction
into reality. It is very easy to make an abstraction from
each action, and in this abstraction to lose the possibility of action. We see constantly that the most real teaching of life is being transmuted by clever rhetoric into
an unapproachable abstraction, and for the appeasing
of the weak will it is being transported into intangible
cloudiness. To make this artificially created abstraction
a reality and substance of life is the next task of Culture. It is impossible for one to imagine that the true
perception of substance, the true teaching of life is only
something forbidding, obstructing, or deadening.

The truth will be there where will be manifested, without obstacles, a constructive broadening containment, and love toward the untiring achievement. Our enemies say that we are forming of ourselves a special race. If we understand by this a nation of culture, then maybe this hostile definition, as too often happens, comes very close to the truth. We shall not be afraid of this truth if, as the highest condemnation, the Black Century, which has already spent itself, will tell us, "Here are gathered dreamers, and they imagine they can help humanity."

Namely, in this help to humanity, we are being reproached. But each of our companions-at-arms, who are scattered all over the world, will smile at that and say: "Does not every natural labor appear to be a help to humanity?" Because it would be abominable to think that everyone who labors does so only for himself. No, he works for someone unknown to him. And this unknown one will accept the nameless labor as an expression of Benevolence, which makes his passage down the earthly path easier for him.

Not dreamers, but embodiments of thoughts; the dream flies away into the shoreless ocean of the air, but the embodiment of thoughts creates substance and cements space with the coming creations. Of the creation of thought into multiple forms, all religions, all teachings have spoken. Many thousands of years before our era, the Egyptians knew the creativeness of thought. And it has been said everywhere, "Thought and Love." And under the sign of the Heart, the Serpent, and the Chalice, in all its multiformity of benevolent symbols, is being given also the wise, preordained inscription "Thought and Love." Because from a thought, an emanation absolutely real, we contrive to make abstractions. We forget that it is not the hand but the thought that creates and kills. And of Love we have made either a sour sigh or an abomination of fornication.

It has been told us that certain branches of the Christian Church recently sanctioned abortion. This unhappy ordinance must be understood as the highest negation of spirituality. Just think, if the Church would recommend murder instead of the wise distribution of strength and abstinence.

If the division of the world into Constructors and Destructors is constantly talked about, then this measure would be a terrible sign of destruction. But Culture, in its essence, does not know destruction as such. It is impetuously, constantly creating; it is constantly covering with a higher dome the imperfections of yesterday. But, here, there is that stone that would be of use to the wise builder, which treats of every possibility.

Verily, in all parts of the world, at present is rising the tension of constructive energy. The lines of new workers cry out: "We are tired of destruction; we are overburdened by senseless mechanization. We want to create; we want to do that useful work that unites us with the resplendent future." In ancient teachings, there has always been pointed out the bridge that unites the old and the new worlds. And nowhere have destruction and violence been mentioned.

If one is to ponder over the spirituality of the future, then this spirituality will be an abstract one but will again return into visibility, into tangibility, and into immutability. And, again, Benevolence will become objective, just as Thought is objective and can be weighed. If one ennobles his life, if instead of vile calumny one tries to turn again to the resplendent creation, is this laughable? Because only ignoramuses will laugh; for them knowledge itself has already become an abstraction, Beauty also has become an unnecessary luxury, and Benevolence itself has become a childish fairy tale. But the most serious scientists long ago came to the conclusion that a fairy tale is a narrative. And a narrative is a historical fact, which one can perceive only through the dust of ages.

The same scientists have pointed out to us that Culture and the achievements of empires have been constructed by Beauty. Take away the monuments of Beauty and the whole aspect of history will be depleted. The virility of Beauty, the age-long inviolability of Culture, tells us of the true transmutation of abstraction into manifested life. And we are not dreamers at all but workers for life, and our apostolate above all is content in that we are striving to say to the people, "Remember Beauty. Do not exile its image from life, but also actively call others to this feast of joy! And if you see allies, do not bid them depart, but find the full measure of benevolent containment in order to call us to the very same peaceful, measureless field of labor and construction. In Beauty and Spirit shall our strength be multiplied. Look into the heights, and spread thy wings as the conqueror of the predestined Light."

In the day of disturbances and tremor, we will repeatedly affirm the very same construction and the same benevolent Light. And there are no conditions that could turn one aside who has entered the path of construction. And we will not be afraid in the name of the Beautiful; and we will remember that the ridicule of ignorance is only a torch of achievement. If we will eschew egotism, if we will strive not only ourselves toward the path of the Beautiful but also by all possible means open it to our nearest ones, then we will have already fulfilled the next task of the enlightening of Culture.

GOODLINESS OF QUALITY

[*The Dawn of India.* Calcutta, Vol. V, No. 10, May, 1944, p. 633]

IN the time of Akbar, it was forbidden under severe penalty to sell perishable colors. Again, the ancient *shastras* speak about the good quality of paints. It would seem that civilization ought to have increased the durability of materials. But civilization aims at other goals. It has abandoned the humanities and forgotten about quality. Certain machine-made products lack durability when compared with those of the past. As to artists' materials, they have had to suffer considerably from *civilization.* Thus, many colors cannot stand the sulfur fumes and other chemical effluvia with which the atmosphere of cities is now filled. Instead of preservation, there is a loss of value. If gasoline fumes on the Paris boulevards have caused the trees to wither, one can imagine how similar emanations can harm people in body and mind. Louis XIV's cynical saying, "After us, the deluge," may well be applied to the contemporary spirit. It is a kind of pharisaism. With a sanctimonious modesty, people will often say: "It is not for us to be concerned whether the art of today is going to last. Let time itself be the judge." Such people know quite well that this is to deprive the coming generations of all that has been done for their sake. Archaeology provides striking examples of the durability of various materials. Should we not be grateful to those workers known to us, thanks to whom we can study and be enraptured by objects that have come down to us through the course of thousands of years?

Some may say that it is certain that the planet will not last for long, that astronomical and cosmic research shows us that earthly materials are not everlasting. Yet so long as the earth exists, one should think of keeping materials in good condition so as to avoid corruption and destruction.

ART-LOVERS

[*The Twentieth Century*. Allahabad, June, 1945, pp. 333–336]

HOW are we to bring art into everyday life? Where are these blessed paths? Perhaps they are inaccessibly difficult? Or they may require countless wealth? Or only spiritual giants may venture along these paths of beauty?

All assurances will be unconvincing. These doubts can be answered only by a page out of real life.

I shall take the portraits of four of my friends. They have all left us now. Only one of them was rich in money; the other three were rich only in the brightness of their spirits.

The rich collector was the Moscow merchant Tretiakov. There was nothing in his family to dispose him toward art. Rather did that old merchant family look with suspicion on the art it did not understand. But, unexpectedly, young Tretiakov was drawn into a new path. And gropingly guided by personal feeling, he began to collect pictures of the Russian school. He went his way alone, only now and again listening to the advice of some artist friend. And it was not by chance that the now-famous Tretiakov Gallery in Moscow began to come into being. With the true intuition of a picture-lover, Tretiakov understood that the government generally filled its museums mostly with official productions, passing over the best work of the artists. And this official physiognomy of the museums could not reflect the evolution of the national school. So has it ever been. And so, I fear, it will be in the future.

Art has always blossomed with an ardent personal urge, which will comprehend and find and preserve and give to the whole nation. And, so, the merchant Tretiakov grasped the national task of art. And he found out fresh artist powers and lightened their path. And he preserved their work, surrounding them with pure delight. But he made his joy a national joy, and while still alive gave the whole of his remarkable collection to the city of Moscow. And the task that he had set for himself was no small one. He had not simply gathered together a mass of valuable pictures but made his collection reflect the whole of the Russian school. Everything that was new, brilliant, important came under the eye of Tretiakov. This taciturn, gray-headed man, in his large fur coat, indefatigably visited all exhibitions, and nothing could hold him when he considered a picture important. He would mount the steep stair leading to the studio of the young beginner in art. He was first to see a picture finished. He was first at the opening of an exhibition. But he was also first in the possession of the best and most characteristic work.

It came to pass that the prizes given by the highest art institutions were considered as naught compared with the purchase of a picture by Tretiakov. And the destiny of the beginner in art was decided not by the Academy but by this sincere and taciturn man. When there was no more room on the walls in his house, Tretiakov built another beside it. If this was needed it had to be done. And art was not to suffer any loss.

Of course, it may be said that with Tretiakov's great wealth it was possible to collect on this vast scale. He was able to choose the best and could gather enough to represent the whole of the Russian school in his collection. It was true that his wealth made this scale possible, but the quality of the collection, his love of the work, and his living creative work in the choice itself of pictures and of men—all this proceeded not from the amount of his means but from the countless riches of his spirit. Thus did one man, strong in spirit, do an infinitely important national work. And now, should the government seek to have a new Tretiakov Gallery, it would find itself powerless, for it was the urge of the spirit that created that inimitable combination of beauty.

This is an instance of ideal creativeness within national limits.

Now for another spiritual portrait. Here we have the same power of spiritual urge along with a mighty struggle with means. It was Count Golenishchev-Kutuzov, a well-known poet and worker in the sphere of culture, and chamberlain at the Imperial Court. In his case, family traditions conduced to the development in him of the love of art. His historical knowledge was great; special deep poetic gifts were his.

His collection consisted of pictures of the old Dutch, Flemish, and Italian schools. Its fundamental characteristic was not the search for conventional names but the truth shown in wonderful creations. The collector understood that the names of Rembrandt, Rubens, Van Dyck are purely collective names, that only the lowest type of collector seeks in the dark for that which to him is but an empty sound. But a better knowledge of art shows us a countless number of artists engulfed in the so-called great names. And the task of the cultured collector is to distinguish among these forgotten names for truth's sake. If on an excellent picture attributed to Rembrandt, we find the signature of Karel Fabricius, his pupil, is a fine picture any the worse for that? Or again, could Van Dyck paint two thousand portraits in one year? Of course not, but he had up to two hundred pupils.

I know how grieved the Count would be to learn

that one of his favorite pictures, by an unknown Flemish painter Hasselaer, now hangs in the Metropolitan Museum in New York under the name of Joachim Patinir.

In the name of truth, Count Golenishchev-Kutuzov sought to discover the real names of painters and remedied, as far as he could, the sins of mercenary human history. And what loving intimacy breathed from his choice collection. Every picture, too, had been obtained with difficulty, with privation. Every new member of the collection was greeted with the disapproval of numerous relations who grudged the money spent on it. And money was so scarce. His small Court salary was not enough to live on. And this collector departed this world surrounded by his real friends, his pictures. And he willed that his collection be dispersed to give new joy to new seeking souls.

Golenishchev-Kutuzov was the type of the refined collector, who, working and rejoicing in new beauty and truth, sends it forth again to serve for the ennobling of the human spirit.

Now for the type of a young collector—an instinctive collector from his school days. Instead of the joys natural to his age, the boy develops a love for works of art. From childhood, without possessing any personal artistic capacities, he is distinguished by education and developed taste. He is attracted by all that is beautiful. His spirit seeks to rise.

"What pleasure it was to pass the time with young Sleptsoff." While yet a pupil of the Imperial Lyceum, he began to collect pictures. His purchases were not chaotic, not accidental. He knew what he was doing. And all money given to the boy by his mother for pleasures was spent on his noble pursuit. And if sometimes he was short of money, his enthusiasm for his general task never suffered from this.

And this general task was a fine one. The boy developed a love for certain very subtly selected painters and decided to have specimens of each of them in all the periods of their work to preserve and to hand on to posterity a complete picture of the creative human life of each. The youth dreamed of the future; each painter was to have a separate room, and the whole furnishing of the room was to correspond with the character of the art represented in it—the furniture, the embellishment of the walls and ceiling, the character of the lighting, and the floor covering. From this we may gather what subtlety of perception lay in that young soul, and what deep love and care surrounded each of the artists represented. In these special rooms, choice singing and music were to be heard at times. Our suitable passages were to be read aloud. In a word the dream of harmony of the unity of art was to be realized.

It was a joy to hear how a new work of art was selected for the collection. What subtle and truthful considerations were expressed for discovering and bringing out a new and worthy feature in the creative work of an artist. And you could see in this treatment of art no mere fancy but a real cultural need. And this subtlety of culture infected those surrounding him. Both thought and speech were purified by this bright ascension of the spirit.

Sleptsov dreamed of handing over his collection to the nation, without any care for his name. But he left us too early to do so. And he left us in an unusual way. He went out for a ride and did not return. He passed over unexpectedly, in the midst of Nature, listening to the harmony of the Cosmos. An enviable passage, a passage to new beautiful labors.

This was the type of a sensitive soul with ingrained feelings of a future harmony and unity.

Now for one more touching type of a collector.

A very poor officer in a line regiment, stationed in a distant, provincial town, reaches out to art with all his soul. Depriving himself of many things. Colonel Kratchkovsky, always pleasant in manner, always active, burning with enthusiasm, seeks to gather a collection of specimens of Russian painting. Of course, he is unable to collect large pictures. So, he collects small pictures, sketches, studies, drawings. But in its essential value, his collection becomes a very considerable one. He seeks for the best painters; he understands that often the sketch is more valuable than the picture itself. He seeks to bring out the character of the artist in its most typical features. This is not a buyer of cheap pictures. This is a true collector. And therewithal he himself is often in want of ten rubles (five dollars), and for him it is a matter of the greatest consequence whether he has to pay ten rubles more or less for a picture. And he asks the painter to let him have the picture, and persistently persuades him to accept a lower price. And his words produced their effects, and the sketches were given to him. And he would rejoice with the bright joy of a child and would write enthusiastic letters about his new treasure. How he loved art, and with what lofty meaning he surrounded the conception of true creative work!

In his will he bequeathed the whole of his collection for public use. More than that, he commanded that all of his modest property, all that he had in daily use, be sold, and the proceeds applied to the purchase of more works of art that were to be added to his collection.

This is the type of an outwardly unnoticed but deeply important worker for the culture of the future. His example drew the attention of many. And if you could see his letters written from the battlefield! His was a pure soul. Colonel Kratchkovsky left us during the late war.

I might show you many more characters, full of

noble seeking in different spheres of art. But even these four types show the level of those cultural aspirations that are so necessary for humanity.

So do things happen; not in dreams but in real life—sincerely and actively. And such pure labors are accompanied by a smile of joy. How near are the seekings of art to the attainment of the spirit.

It is time to understand, to note, and to apply these wondrous channels to life.

And when art has entered actively, irresistibly, and simply into all spiritual development of public life, then it will also be brought into the whole of modern life.

And it is through these channels that the true paths of blessing will draw near to every human heart.

MAHAGURU

[*Our India*. New Delhi, Vol. I, No. 4, October, 1946, p. 123]

A S a Light-bearing Beacon upon the rock of nonviolence stands Gandhi, the Mahaguru of Bharata.

Glorious ploughman on the vast field of Culture! Him, admired by the whole world.

He brings into everyday life the Amrita of Culture. He kindles innumerable torches of Self-sacrificing Spirits.

He untiringly remains on the Watchtower, and no storm can interrupt His blessed Vigil. He guards the treasures of India.

He strives for Cultural Unity, as for panhuman Panacea. He knows that real Peace can abide only in the Realm of Beauty and Harmony.

Mahaguru, to Thee my invocation and reverence. Long live the Hero of Bharata.

Himalayas,
September 9, 1946.

HAIL BHARATA!

[*Silpi*. Madras, Vol. I, No. 3, October, 1946, p. 1]

ON memorable days, one should always think about those matters that should not be forgotten. During the days of the hard, material world crisis, let us look back on the causes that originated such widespread calamity. One should have expected that the discoveries and the inventions of the last years should have given humanity new, unusual possibilities. The means of communications, submarines and ships, underground and overground railways, and all aircraft render their services for speedy interexchange, and, it would seem, for an unheard-of, intense activity.

But instead of expected welfare, we find everywhere disaster and misfortune. In the apparently most prosperous countries, terrifying, huge armies of many millions of unemployed gather. What joy it could bring to humanity by the abovementioned, multifarious ways of communication?

Let us weigh in mind the transported goods; is there amongst the merchandise allotted a sufficient and dignified place for true spiritual values? It has been said, and repeated over again, "Man cannot live on bread alone!" And if humanity has been given such unusual facilities of transportation and communication, then, first of all, they should carry spiritual treasures. Those treasures by which the most powerful countries were formed. Those treasures that created the beautiful epochs of the renaissance, of the rebirth of the highest culture, before which, at present, our hearts enthusiastically tremor.

If we do not recall again those great treasures of the spirit, then what bottomless darkness would be our goal! But let us not forget that difficulties always contain in themselves great possibilities. And the most difficult material hardships always give an impulse toward true spiritual search and achievements; then constructive solutions of seemingly unsolvable problems will descend on mankind as a beautiful light-bearing Messenger of Cultural Unity.

Teachings foresee also difficulties, but after them is always predicted a radiant era. May this change not remain abstract, but may it fertilize the creative thinking of humanity, uplifting it on wings toward positive constructiveness.

Near glorious, ancient sites, we see already new structures, new attainments, and we know how much is pre-destined, and, verily, every year brings for Bharata the Great Victory. "Peace to all beings." May this command not remain in the air and abstract, but may it blossom like a flame, with silverish lotus petals, innumerable, as is the number of striving hearts.

Satyam, Shivam, Sundaram.

REVERING TRUE VALUES

[*East & West.* Hyderabad, Vol. XIX, No. 2,
September, 1947, p. 35]

LET everyone in his field, within his possibilities, apply his strength and experience to affirm urgently the sign of peaceful cooperation. No obstacles, no convulsions of hatred and falsehood, can prevent humanity from striving toward the reverence of true values. The measure of destruction and vandalism is overflowing. Nobody will dare say that this is an exaggeration. Murder, slander, destruction take place daily. The shameful, black foam of hatred fills the earth. The heart of humanity, of course, realizes that one cannot proceed further by this path. The whispering of hypocrites that "the situation is not bad" is not convincing for those who see with their own eyes all the horrors around them, not only at times of war but also at all other times, which through some misunderstanding are called times of peace. The human heart wants real peace. It strives to labor—creatively and actively. It wants to love and expand in the realization of Sublime Beauty. In the highest perception of Beauty and Knowledge, all conventional divisions disappear. The heart speaks its own language; it wants to rejoice at that which is common for all, uplifts all, and leads to the radiant Future.

www.ingramcontent.com/pod-product-compliance
Lightning Source LLC
Chambersburg PA
CBHW071544030726
47598CB00001B/222